Volume 5

THE WORLD'S
ECONOMIC FUTURE

THE WORLD'S ECONOMIC FUTURE

A. LOVEDAY, J. B. CONDLIFFE,
B. OHLIN, E. F. HECKSCHER
AND
S. DE MADARIAGA

Routledge
Taylor & Francis Group

LONDON AND NEW YORK

First published in 1938 by George Allen & Unwin Ltd.

This edition first published in 2025
by Routledge
4 Park Square, Milton Park, Abingdon, Oxon OX14 4RN

and by Routledge
605 Third Avenue, New York, NY 10158

Routledge is an imprint of the Taylor & Francis Group, an informa business

British Library Cataloguing in Publication Data
A catalogue record for this book is available from the British Library

ISBN: 978-1-032-88942-9 (Set)
ISBN: 978-1-032-88062-4 (Volume 5) (hbk)
ISBN: 978-1-032-88074-7 (Volume 5) (pbk)
ISBN: 978-1-003-53608-6 (Volume 5) (ebk)

DOI: 10.4324/9781003536086

Publisher's Note
The publisher has gone to great lengths to ensure the quality of this reprint but points out that some imperfections in the original copies may be apparent.

Disclaimer
The publisher has made every effort to trace copyright holders and would welcome correspondence from those they have been unable to trace.

This book is a re-issue originally published in 1938. The language used and views portrayed are a reflection of its era and no offence is meant by the Publishers to any reader by this re-publication.

THE

SIR HALLEY STEWART TRUST

★

FOUNDED 15TH DECEMBER 1924
FOR RESEARCH TOWARDS THE CHRISTIAN IDEAL IN ALL
SOCIAL LIFE.

The objects of the Trust are *in general:*

To advance religion; to advance education; to relieve poverty; to promote other Charitable purposes beneficial to the community, and *in particular:*

1. To assist in the discovery of the best means by which "the mind of Christ" may be applied to extending the Kingdom of God by the prevention and removal of human misery;

2. To assist in the study of our Lord's life and teaching in their explicit and implicit application to the social relationships of man;

3. To express the mind of Christ in the realization of the Kingdom of God upon earth and in a national and a world-wide brotherhood;

For example:

For every Individual, by furthering such favourable opportunities of education, service, and leisure as shall enable him or her most perfectly to develop the body, mind, and spirit:

In all Social Life, whether domestic, industrial, or national, by securing a just environment, and

In International Relationships, by fostering good will between all races, tribes, peoples, and nations so as to secure the fulfilment of the hope of "peace on earth";

4. To provide fees for a Lecture or Lectures annually and prizes for essays or other written compositions, and to pay for their publication and distribution;

5. To provide, maintain, and assist Lectures and Research work in Social, Economic, Psychological, Medical, Surgical, or Educational subjects;

6. To make grants to Libraries;

7. To assist publications exclusively connected with the objects of the Trust (not being newspapers or exclusively denominational);

8. To make grants to and co-operate with Societiess, Organizations, and Persons engaged in the furtherance of Charitable objects similar to the objects of the Trust;

9. To use the foregoing and any such other method, whether of a like nature or not, as are lawful and reasonable and appropriate for the furtherance of the objects of the Trust.

The income of the Trust may not be used for dogmatic, theological or ecclesiastical purposes other than the cult of the Science of God as manifest in man in the Son of Man in the person and teaching of our Lord, "The Word of God," Who "liveth and abideth forever."

SIR HALLEY STEWART LECTURES, 1937

THE
WORLD'S ECONOMIC FUTURE

by

A. Loveday, M.A.

Director, League of Nations
Economics Intelligence Service

J. B. Condliffe, D.Sc., M.A.

Professor of Commerce
London University

B. Ohlin

Professor of Economics
Stockholm University

E. F. Heckscher

Professor of Economic History
Stockholm University

S. de Madariaga, M.A. (Oxon.)

Late Spanish Representative
League of Nations Council

With an Introduction by
D. H. Robertson, M.A.

LONDON
George Allen & Unwin Ltd
MUSEUM STREET

FIRST PUBLISHED IN 1938

CONTENTS

		PAGE
INTRODUCTION		11
by D. H. Robertson, M.A.		

I. PROBLEMS OF ECONOMIC INSECURITY   17
   by A. Loveday

II. THE DISTRIBUTION OF POWER AND
    LEADERSHIP   43
    by Professor J. B. Condliffe, D.Sc., M.A.

III. ON THE FUTURE ECONOMIC ORGANI-
     ZATION OF SOCIETY   65
     by B. Ohlin

IV. RECENT TENDENCIES IN ECONOMIC
    LIFE   87
    by Professor E. F. Heckscher

V. MENTAL SETTINGS OF OUR ECONOMIC
   FUTURE   110
   by S. de Madariaga, M.A.

INTRODUCTION

by

D. H. ROBERTSON

I⊤ is a high privilege to be asked to show the audience to their seats for a rehearing of this fine series of lectures; yet not altogether an enviable one. For in what need does such a galaxy of artistes stand of a garrulous *compère*? Each lecture is already a model of condensed argument, so that to attempt further summarization would be impertinent. And, in spite of each contributor's independence of judgment and of some differences of emphasis, there pervades the series a broad unity of outlook and temper, so that elaborate attempts to "compare and contrast," in the manner to which the setters of examination papers invite us, would be out of place.

What seems to me to give special value to the series is the way in which analysis and speculation are made to grow out of strict attention to the facts of the contemporary world. The lecturers' heads are in the stars, but their feet are on the earth. Their purpose is to throw light on the fundamental problems of human society—the relation of the individual to the national State in which he finds himself embedded, the relation of the national State to the whole body of mankind, and—perhaps most elusive problem of all—the relation between these two relations. But they discuss these high matters not in terms of airy generalities, but in the light of the needs of the men and women of to-day, as conditioned by the way in which things have actually happened during the last few decades of human history.

It may perhaps assist the reader towards forming his own synthesis of the lectures if I first set out baldly the three basic facts to which abundant allusion is made in them, and then proceed to illustrate how they have served the lecturers as starting-points for forceful argument and illuminating suggestion. These facts are the increased dependence of man for his economic welfare on expensive and durable instruments; the check to the growth of population in the western world; and the diffusion of economic power over the globe.

(1) It is above all the superior technical effectiveness of large-scale production and transport which has compelled the greater *centralization* of the powers of economic control and decision, whether in the hands of private or public bodies (Professor Ohlin), and which indeed, in the form of the railway, began to threaten the " atomistic" assumptions of early nineteenth-century liberalism almost as soon as they had been formulated (Professor Heckscher). (There are, however, thanks to the motor vehicle and the transmission of electric power, some signs of a backwash in this respect; but it is not clear how much significance we can legitimately attach to them—there are, I think, traces of an amicable difference of opinion between the two distinguished

Swedes in this regard.) The solution is not necessarily an extension of Government operation over the whole industrial field, but a system "which combines flexibility with the possibility of centralized direction in certain special respects" (Professor Ohlin).

But this same prominence of the fixed capital instrument, capable when once created of satisfying demand for many years, has made economic progress more discontinuous, and the tenure of opportunities for employment more insecure. And the State, having stepped in to temper this insecurity for the individual, has become itself intensely conscious of the risks of fluctuation, and been driven to improvise methods of averting or minimizing them. In its first phase this new development has led to an intensification of economic nationalism; but it may be predicted that it will in the end help to compel the recognition of the need for an international order (Mr. Loveday).

(2) The check to the growth of population also increases the "bumpiness" of economic life, and that in various ways. Demand turns away from the bread and butter which little Tommy is only too obviously ready to wolf day by day, and the stockings which he has only too obviously worn out, to the motor-car and the gramophone which Papa and Mamma must save for in the first instance, but which, once bought, can be made to do another year (Mr. Loveday). Problems of excess capacity develop, on a scale unknown to the expansive nine-

teenth century, and call for centralized handling; yet the removal of the dynamic force of population growth only enhances the need to keep alive that other great dynamic force—individual enterprise and initiative (Professor Ohlin). But stay!—are we falling too ready victims to that "decline of optimism" which Professor Ohlin diagnoses as one of the causes of increased reliance on collective action? Here is Professor Condliffe ready to call in an Old World to redress the balance of the New. Perhaps there will be a new cycle of growth in the great peasant populations of the Far East; and perhaps that will set a new task and offer a new hope to the flagging enterprise and industry of Western Europe.

(3) Perhaps—but perhaps not. For the Japanese have other ideas—and so perhaps have the Chinese themselves. Further, the centre of gravity has shifted—westward, as throughout the ages. Can it fail to settle definitively in the United States, with her enormous resources and her favoured geographical position? And here we come round again to the bearing of physical facts on the two fundamental social problems—the Individual and the Nation—the Nation and the World. For the rise towards leadership of the United States looks like making life bumpier for the rest of us, and so strengthening the forces compelling State intervention in the economic field. And it places outside the sole power of Great Britain the re-creation of that pre-war international economic order which was in such large measure a British order, and

compels us forward on the paths of international co-operation.

This third subject is Professor Condliffe's special province; and in alluding to it I have come near to suffering the fate which I feared—that of degenerating from showman into précis-writer. But in truth here as elsewhere I have rather selected than summarized. For these three basic influences—technological, biological, geographical—breed and interbreed in the lecturers' minds to give rise to a whole family of thoughts relevant to those two main issues of how man must behave with man, and nation with nation, if the potentialities of individual well-being now within our grasp are not to be stillborn through defects of organization or poured away in civil or external warfare.

And at least I have not made, and shall not make, any attempt to epitomize that scintillating lecture by Señor Madariaga which, even if it were not the last in the book, I should advise the reader to keep till the end. For if he is feeling even a little jaded (though I hope he will not have had time to be) with birth-rates and occupational distributions and cartels, it will exhilarate him the more to be caught up in Señor Madariaga's fiery chariot, whirled across the borders which delimit the Knowledge of Man from the Knowledge of Nature and the Knowledge of Knowledge Itself, and (after pausing here and there to prick a bubble or dethrone a dogma) set down again in the heart of the twofold problem—the Individual and the Nation, the Nation and the World.

And so we close the book, and take up our daily newspaper. What is to be done about herrings? About the coal-mines? About renters' quotas and exhibitors' quotas? About the text of the League Covenant, and the administration of Tanganyika and Shanghai? Have we been told? Perhaps not. But perhaps at least we shall return to the consideration of these and similar matters with minds fresher and sharper—less flecked with vinegar or muffled with wool.

D. H. ROBERTSON

WORLD'S ECONOMIC FUTURE

I

PROBLEMS OF ECONOMIC INSECURITY

by A. Loveday

THIS course of lectures is intended to deal with various aspects of the economic future. Now the difficulty of interpreting the past or of understanding what is happening around us to-day in this world that seems to be dominated by everything but reason is so great that no prudent person would commit himself willingly and wittingly to prophecies about events to come. You will not, I trust, therefore, expect me to paint a word picture of some unseen horizon.

The most that can be attempted—and that itself is perhaps unduly venturesome—is to consider some of the forces that have driven recent events into the course along which they have flowed, and to endeavour to estimate their probable strength in the future. We must confine ourselves to fundamental forces that do not spring from collective or controlled human will, and that are not themselves easily affected by changes in political beliefs or in political dogmas willingly or unwillingly accepted. I propose to select for consideration three such fundamental forces or factors all of which, I think, tend to render society more sensitive to fluctuations in economic activity. But before I enumerate them I want to give a word of explanation about the reasons for my choice.

We are living to-day in a world from which the sense of the fitness of things—the sense of normalcy —has departed. Each one of us is suffering consciously or subconsciously from a feeling of political, social, and economic insecurity. Incident succeeds incident, depression depression, crisis crisis; and even when for some brief period the ship of State moves on an even keel, or even when the economic prospects of the immediate future seem brighter than the retrospect of the immediate past, there remains a foreboding of political or economic disaster in one part of the world or in another at some date approximate enough to appal. There is more than foreboding; there is a constantly present and widespread feeling of the incompatibility of the individual with his environment; a feeling by the individual that what he wants above all is rest and security, the possibility of merging himself in his environment and finding, not in somnolence, but in reasoned activity, tranquillity, and that what he finds is an environment shifting, unstable, incomprehensible. This regnant and universal insecurity is attributed widely and somewhat vaguely to the shocks caused by the war, or to this or that political arrangement, political movement, or political ambition.

I do not propose to attempt to unravel the manifold causal threads that must be traced over their individual lengths before we can understand the complex fragility of the world which constitutes our environment to-day. But I believe that this fragility, and our own sense of insecurity, are due in part at least—indeed, to an important degree—to certain economic factors over which we have acquired but limited control and to which we have given insufficient recognition. I select these factors for consideration not because I believe that they must necessarily prove dominant in the future, but because they are, I believe, potent contributory causes to-day of the most serious of our present ills—collective economic insecurity.

To what extent they will prove dominant in the future no one can foresee. Forces quite unknown to us may arise and radically change economic life. Populations may be decimated by some hitherto unknown or relatively harmless disease; processes may be discovered for employing the force from an exploded atom or harnessing the tides; methods may be elaborated—have perhaps already been elaborated —for producing our food requirements at reduced costs without the use of soil; the centres of economic gravity through one discovery or another may be altered: moreover, there is the risk of war, and what the effects may be of another war in Europe on a scale comparable to that of the last no one can foresee.

There is thus no certainty that—quite apart from war—the forces which are determinant to-day will be dominant to-morrow. But I doubt myself whether the influence of those economic factors which are contributing to collective insecurity at this moment will become less apparent as the effects of the last war fade in the distance. They will become less apparent as ways and means are found to control them.

I propose, as I have said, to select three factors which tend—as I see it—to contribute to economic insecurity largely because they tend to increase the probability of economic depressions occurring, or because they tend to render them more intense. But I do not propose to elaborate any sort of theory of what is known as the trade cycle. I am concerned here with factors or forces which affect the whole structure of society within which the trade cycle operates and renders that structure more susceptible to fluctuations in economic activity, however those fluctuations may be caused.

The three factors that I have in mind are the following:

(a) The drop or arrest in the rate of growth of the populations of Western Europe and of certain other parts of the world enjoying what we call a western civilization.

(b) The increase in the average income per head of population—especially in these areas—which for all the ups and downs of booms and depressions, and despite all the destruction of war, and waste on preparations for war, has continued steadily for the last hundred and fifty years and still continues.

(c) The increase in the capitalistic processes of

production, by which I mean the system of indirect production—the ultimate consumers' product being manufactured not directly by man's hands and simple tools, but as the result of a long series of mechanical processes.

Capitalistic processes as just defined are, I should perhaps add, not necessarily more characteristic of what is called capitalist economy than of a socialist or communist economy. The economic distinction between capitalism and communism depends primarily upon the differences in the rights to the ownership of capital, not on whether production is to a greater or less extent effected with the use of capital goods, that is machinery and plant.

I have selected these three factors in part because they all seem to me to have a profound influence on our economic life and problems to-day, but especially because they are all, I venture to think, likely to continue as active phenomena in the future. The second and the third—the increase in the income per head of population, and the increase of capitalistic processes of production—may, it is true, succumb to the destructive influences of war—but knowledge of mechanical and scientific processes is now so widespread throughout the world that the risk of a return to barbarism is infinitely less than it has been in any other civilization.

I. POPULATION FACTOR

As you are all no doubt aware, the birth rate in this country has been falling steadily for the last sixty years,[1] and such increase in population as has taken place since 1876 has been wholly due to a reduction in the death rate. But there is a point beyond which the death rate cannot fall, and the prospects in this country are that in quite a few years, probably before 1945, the population will have reached its maximum and will thereafter decline —at first slowly. In other parts of industrial Europe the situation is similar. According to Professor Carr-Saunders "we may anticipate that in north and west Europe there will be no further increase of population of any importance, and that before 1950 population will be on the decline in most countries in this region. But in no case will the decline be large twenty years from now."[2]

This tendency towards population stability and subsequent decline is not peculiar to Europe; it is common to all countries with what we call a western civilization, with the exception of certain European agricultural States and one or two others.

Thus Professor Carr-Saunders considers it probable "that although, in the absence of immigration, population will continue to grow in the United States, Australia, New Zealand, and non-French Canada, the maximum population will not be more than 10–15 per cent larger than the present population."[3]

In the agricultural States of Eastern and South-

---

[1] It began to fall in 1876.
[2] *World Population*, p. 135, by A. M. Carr-Saunders, Clarendon Press, 1936.   [3] Op. cit., p. 179.

Eastern Europe, on the other hand, where the death rate is still high, there is every reason to expect a large, and indeed with the steady improvement in social hygiene, a rapid increase in population, resulting not from a rise in the birth rate, but from a fall in the death rate. Throughout the nineteenth century the declining death rate has been the efficient cause in Europe of population growth.

I am mainly concerned in this lecture with the probable effects of the tendency towards population stability or decline; but, as I shall endeavour to show, the fact that agricultural populations are likely to continue to grow removes what might otherwise have been one possible means of diminishing the economic instability which threatens the more highly industrialized regions of the world.

Why should a stable or declining population be subject to greater economic insecurity than a growing population? At first sight one might be inclined to assume that the greater the proportion of children in any population, since they are the least able to fend for themselves, the greater would be the chance of this or that adverse economic factor causing disaster. Indeed, this may be true; but population stability or decline for all that gives rise to changes in the whole nature of consumption and in the structure of production which renders society peculiarly vulnerable to economic depressions.

This weakness is caused, in the first instance, by the influence of population stability on demand. When a population is growing rapidly a large proportion of the total demand for goods and services is composed of demand for immediately consumable necessities such as food, or necessities with a more or less strictly limited life such as clothes—especially children's clothes—boots and shoes, and for services, such as education, which must continue to be rendered in good and bad times alike.

In a stable or declining population the proportion of children is less—the family is small and more is spent on durable goods, such as houses, electric power in one form or another, motor cars, radio sets, refrigerators, central heating installations, etc. More is spent also on services which can be forgone. When business is bad we all spend less on theatres and restaurants, and on travel, and in doing so make business worse.

Demand changes, therefore, from goods which are first essential and secondly of short life to goods which are not essential and are relatively durable; it shifts from services which are essential to services which are not.

In two ways does this shift in demand lead to greater economic uncertainty. One I have just mentioned. Because the goods composing what I may call secondary demand are not essential to existence or to a standard of living which under almost any circumstances will be maintained, the public will, when economic conditions tend for one reason or another to become less favourable, begin to economize on their purchases and in so doing increase the incipient depression by throwing out of employment those who were occupied in making those goods or rendering those services. Moreover, the public can draw in its horns all the more easily because, in fact, it does not have to deprive itself altogether of the satisfactions it derives from goods satisfying secondary needs when it abstains for a time from purchasing them. These goods, as I have said, are in general of a more durable nature than consumption goods; a public intent on effecting economies continues to enjoy its houses, its motor cars, its furniture, and its household equipment; only it enjoys the old ones it already possesses instead of new ones on which, in moments of jovial prosperity, it had looked covetously.

Total demand has thus become more sensitive to the general economic temperature; business becomes more uncertain; economic life more bumpy.

But business is more uncertain for another reason. Secondary demand is much more difficult to estimate than the demand for essential food and clothing. It is possible to estimate the number of boots or shoes, that really are boots or shoes and not simply decorative elegancies, likely to be required in any year from the number of the population, and the annual increase in demand from the annual increase in the population of boot-wearing age. But by what means other than that of trial and error can one estimate the demand for cameras? The risk of error in business anticipation is thus increased and more occasions are likely to arise of excess production and unsaleable stocks, or alternatively of demand outstripping the immediately available capacity to produce and giving rise to the need for a sudden expansion of plant; and by the time the new plant is constructed, the demand may have changed owing to a change in fashion or the marketing of some other commodity which appeals momentarily to popular taste. Secondary demand is thus at once peculiarly sensitive to changes in the economic atmosphere, eclectic and fickle as fashion is fickle.

II. INCOME FACTOR

Some of you will say that the changes in demand that I have attributed to stable or relatively stable population might equally well or, indeed, better have been attributed to increasing wealth per head of population; that in any society which is growing richer a point will sooner or later be reached at which primary demand is largely satisfied and there is a growing surplus of income for the satisfaction of secondary demand. That, to a large extent, is true. But it is difficult to estimate the extent to which increasing wealth or income per head of population is due to a fall in population (or to a fall in its rate of increase) and how far it is due to all that complex of more direct economic factors on which economic progress in the narrow sense of the term depends.

Moreover, though the effect of the two factors is similar and though they combine to intensify each other, they are distinct and may each act independently. Thus, even were income per head in any country not increasing, the composition of that country's total demand would be influenced if population was becoming stationary. For in such a population there would be fewer children and more persons of middle age. Less would therefore be spent on, for instance, food and clothes for children and more on durable goods for their elders.

The obverse is true. Once a certain level of comfort has been reached, an increase of income will tend to shift demand to more durable goods and to services, even when population is growing also. The more rapid the growth of income relatively to that population, the stronger this tendency will be.

We may consider these two factors, then, of declining population (or declining rate of increase) and increasing income per head as at once independent and interdependent, and producing both severally and jointly the result of greater economic bumpiness and hence uncertainty, which I have just endeavoured to describe.

III. CAPITALISTIC PROCESSES OF PRODUCTION

The third factor that I mentioned just now was the growth of the capitalistic processes of production, by which I stated that I meant an increase in the indirectness of production, the commodity which is intended for sale to the final purchaser, requiring for its production the investment of capital in other plant or tools with which to make it.

Now the fact that a large proportion of the goods produced in any society are produced thus indirectly with the aid of costly plant on which much labour has previously been expended has an influence on the smooth working of the whole economic system very similar to the fact that society expends a relatively large proportion of its income on durable goods. For again, when for one reason or another business prospects look less bright than they did shortly before, when there is some drop in the rate of growth of the demand for goods by the public, the business man will contract his demand for new machines and new plant and continue to satisfy this slightly flagging demand with his existing plant. The greater the proportion of the total demand for goods in any community met by means of what I call capitalistic processes, the greater the risk of a contraction in the demand for plant seriously affecting general economic activity. This is obvious, for if, for instance, there is in any country a large number of people employed in good times on making plant —on capital industries—and the demand for plant suddenly drops—many of these people will be thrown out of employment and the depression will thus spread.

Demand may be looked upon as appertaining to a series of overlapping groups of goods and services, with absolute necessities at one end of the scale and new capital goods at the other; between these two we find conventional necessities, goods satisfying secondary needs, luxuries, etc. At each step demand becomes less and less stable. There is a physiological check to the contraction of the demand for food, there are conventional checks to the contraction of demand for other goods, conventional checks which become weaker and weaker the more durable the goods are. The demand for plant may fall to zero. In so far as it consists of a demand for new plant, not simply replacement, it may fall to zero when the demand for consumption goods is maintained unaltered but has ceased to grow. Thus a change, not in the total amount of the demand for consumption goods, but in the rate of growth of that demand, may cause a complete or almost complete cessation in the demand for additional capital goods in the narrow sense of that term.

All the three factors I have selected for consideration therefore tend to operate in the same way. They tend to render total demand more sensitive and the rhythm of economic activity less smooth.

The more total demand and consequently total productive resources are devoted to satisfying needs which are not considered to be of first necessity, the greater the possible contraction of demand and of productive activity, the more serious our depressions are likely to be.

By this I do not mean that future depressions will on the average be more intense than that through which we have just passed. We may at least hope that they will be less intense; for there were special causes contributing to the depression which started in 1929 which, granted peace—or, I should say, the limitation of the range of warfare—are not likely to recur, and there are reasons to anticipate that the long-term trend of prices in the future will be upwards. The evidence of the past goes to show that when this is the case depressions are less intense than when the long-term trend of prices is downwards.

But the three factors I have been considering will, I think, whatever the course of prices in the future, render society more susceptible to changes in the economic temperature. They will tend to cause in the future, unless means to counter their natural influence are devised, as they are causing to-day, a widespread feeling of economic insecurity, and through their direct effects and indirectly through the feeling of insecurity to which they give rise, profoundly influence our destinies and economic policy in the future.

In what way are they likely to influence our destinies or future policy? To answer that question we must first consider the nature of the risks that this tendency towards economic bumpiness which I foresee, entails. These risks are not, I think, the same as the economic risks that the average working man or the average shareholder had to brace himself to meet from time to time a hundred or even fifty years ago.

Certain economic changes of major importance have taken place.

First, the risk of depressions causing physical, as distinct from mental, suffering is less than it was. The measures taken by the great majority of industrial States to ensure the worker against the risk of starvation when work and wages are no longer available to him, or to assure him medical assistance in ill-health, have removed, not the fear of misery but the fear of death from want.

In more primitive times individual economic insecurity, the risk of being left not only without work but also without means of subsistence, the risk of dying of starvation, or spending one's whole life in a state of semi-starvation, was incomparably greater than it is to-day. To-day in modern industrial States risks have been largely socialized. The whole productive community is more subject to violent upheavals of economic equilibrium; but in the worst of depressions the risk to the individual of being unable to satisfy at least his physiological needs is less than it was half a century ago in good times or bad.

On the other hand, the risk to the individual worker of becoming unemployed has increased. It has increased, if the foregoing analysis is correct, because the factors contributing to variations in economic activity have grown in force. It has increased no doubt also because of the very measures that Governments have taken—and rightly taken—to reduce the suffering consequent upon unemployment. The average employer was naturally more reluctant to dismiss his hands when he knew that those he threw out of work would be in danger of starvation than he is to-day, when measures to which he himself has contributed have been taken to support the unemployed. Any falling-off in business is therefore more likely to result in unemployment to-day than it was formerly. The State has intervened and undertaken, under defined conditions, to assume itself part of the financial risks resulting from variations in economic activity.

Risks have thus been collectivized. That is the third great change, and it is of fundamental importance in any consideration of probable future policy, because it has rendered Governments community-risk conscious.

This community risk is not only financial but also social. Governments which guarantee incomes—however small—when opportunity for work is lacking are naturally anxious for financial reasons to revive employment as rapidly as possible. At the same time they are morally concerned because they have tacitly or overtly assumed a responsibility to take measures to lessen unemployment. They are concerned, too, because of the mental suffering caused by unemployment and by the feeling of insecurity to which economic depressions give rise.

The gravest individual risk—the risk of inability to maintain existence—has diminished for two distinct reasons. First, because with the growth of wealth, it is easier to provide what is indispensable for all; secondly, because the State has taken measures to protect the individual against at least some of the risks of work and some of the tragedy of unemployment.

The collective risk of suffering violent changes in economic activity will not be lessened by greater average prosperity, greater average income per head.

On the contrary, if my argument is correct, that risk will grow as income expands.

What, then, may we expect of the future?

When public opinion, and, through it, Governments, became conscious of the nature of the economic risks to the individual, action was taken by the State and various means of assurance against those risks were devised.

States are to-day becoming conscious of the collective risks and are seeking ways and means to avert them.

Can States insure themselves against the collective risks? I do not think we know the answer to that question to-day, but the endeavour by Governments to find ways and means will, I think, largely determine the general nature, not only of economic policy but also of the economic structure.

There are two ways open. The one is to endeavour to find the causes of economic depressions and the means to prevent those causes becoming operative. That is the course that we have been pursuing at Geneva. We are conducting research into the nature of economic depressions in the hope that sooner or later we may be able to throw some more light on the problem of causation, and thus aid those whose duty it is to formulate constructive policy. We have begun by analysing the theories of trade cycles now currently credited by one school of thought or another, with a view to rendering the real points of difference and the concealed points of agreement clearer. That done, we are now subjecting these diverse theories, so far as possible, to the test of fact, and especially statistical fact. This is a piece of work to which I personally attach great importance, because depressions, through the misery they create, through the mystery of their cause, through the fatalism and the antagonisms to which they give rise, are, I believe, the greatest social danger and the greatest danger to peace and collective sanity and security to which the modern world is subject.

That is the one possible procedure, and it is being followed not, of course, by the League alone, but by groups of scientific thinkers all over the globe. If it succeeds, we may look with much greater confidence not only to the economic but to the political future. It is uncertainty, misgiving, doubt, lack of understanding, ignorance, that lead to discord and jealousy and war. But we can no more be certain that it will succeed, or that it will succeed within any given period of time, than we can be certain that we shall find the cause and cure for cancer within any given period of time.

The statesman will not wait for the research student. Public opinion will not permit him, and these three factors, population stability, increasing wealth per head of population, and the growth of capitalistic processes of production, though not themselves the causes of depressions, will drive him —are driving him—to take more or less empirical action, because of the extent to which they accentuate, and will, I believe, accentuate them. What is the nature of that action likely to be? What action is being taken to-day?

It is obviously not possible to attempt to enumerate all the measures that Governments have adopted in recent years. Nor is it necessary for my purpose, because I only want to consider in the broadest way the general nature of the policies that may be pursued. Almost any of the numerous devices that have been adopted either to render society less susceptible to fluctuations in economic activity or to restart economic activity once it has slowed down will serve to illustrate the points I want to make. I choose three almost at random. First, the attempt to reduce the importance of the capitalistic (indirect) processes of production; secondly, the attempt to spread risks by the diversification of economic activities; and thirdly, the attempt to substitute at certain times collective demand for a waning individual demand.

The first and second of these three lines of policy are, it is true, not clearly distinct. Agriculture is protected to-day in a number of countries in part to diversify production—rather than to increase it; but in part also because in countries where agriculture is not conducted on an industrial basis, it is thought that in good times and bad the agriculturist will remain occupied—the social risks resulting from unemployment are reduced. This protection of agriculture reflects *inter alia* a half-unconscious reaction to the growth of the capitalistic processes of production, a half-blind attempt to remove a greater part of the population from the more indirect to the more direct methods of producing wealth. It may or may not be wise. Its significance lies in the fact that it attaches greater importance to security than to maximum income. A social risk premium is being paid.

Similarly, the growth of industrial protection in recent years is looked upon as an insurance against risks. Governments in industrial States have endeavoured to protect themselves against what was considered excessive specialization in part because industries suffer in unlike degree in periods of depression, and because recovery takes place earlier in some industries than in others. Reciprocally agricultural States protect industry, partly because their populations are growing, and they wish to provide employment for their surplus land workers, and partly because they fear that in bad times raw materials and foodstuffs will fall so much in price that they will be unable to purchase abroad the manufactured goods they require.

Now the growth of protection in agricultural and mining countries which seems to me almost inevitable, or the growth of industry which will quite certainly happen as populations increase and knowledge of industrial arts spreads, will affect the nature of the exports and the production of industrial States. The younger countries, as we call them, will concentrate, are concentrating, in the first place on the manufacture of non-durable consumers' goods, prepared foods, clothing, and later on certain classes of durable consumers' goods such as furniture, house fittings, etc. As this tendency develops the exports of industrial countries tend to be composed to an ever-increasing extent of more expensive durable consumers' goods and capital goods. But as I have endeavoured to show, the fluctuations in the demand for this type of goods must inevitably be greater than the fluctuations in the demand for consumers' goods. While the countries with growing populations and a relatively young industry, especially the mining countries, may to some extent and in certain conditions help to even out these fluctuations by setting up consumers' goods industries, the risks to the older industrial countries are increased. They are increased, you will observe, not only because the stable populations of the industrialized States are becoming richer, but also because the populations in their former markets are not stable but growing. The absence of growth in their own populations tends to shift demand from consumption goods with a short life to durable consumption goods; the growth of population in less advanced countries stimulates the production of consumption goods locally and tends to concentrate demand abroad on capital goods and, for a time, durable consumers' goods. Diversification, therefore, while it may help to spread the risks in each country that applies it as a system of insurance against risk, will not, if applied widely, solve the problem for highly industrialized States.

The third line of policy widely adopted during the recent depression has been the creation of social demand to fill the gap caused by the temporary fading of individual demand. This is the policy of increasing Government expenditure during bad times, generally on one form or another of public works.

I am not concerned here with its merits or demerits, any more than with the merits or demerits of the attempts to arrest the advance of mechanical means of production or to diversify risks. The system of stimulating business activity by Government expenditure has in certain countries become an accepted principle of long-term economic policy. Thus in Finland a special reserve is being built up (which is sterilized in good times) intended for employment by the Government when business slackens, in order to inject new life—additional purchasing power—into the community. If this system of creating anti-depression reserves develops or if Governments which have paid for their public works by borrowing can amortize their debt during the years of prosperity, the policy of adjusting public works programmes to the cycle may become widely accepted. But it is obvious that the system cannot be maintained indefinitely if each depression results in a large addition to the total Government debt.

Government measures to counter the effects of depressions have not, of course, been confined to these three types of policy that I have considered. Some Governments have taken the whole banking and credit system under their control, some have deliberately devaluated their currencies, others have had devaluation forced on them. What direct credit or currency manipulations may be resorted to on the occurrence either of minor depressions or of such catastrophic slumps as that of 1929–32 it is clearly impossible to foresee.

Indeed, I should be walking blindfold into the pitfalls of prophecy of which I spoke at the very beginning of this lecture, if I tried to speculate on the various measures to which Governments may have recourse in their endeavours to avert or mitigate depressions.

It is not my object to give you even a select list of probable starters. I want only to consider the nature of the problem itself with which Governments are faced, and will I think be faced. The three particular lines of policy adopted in the past that I have just mentioned will serve to illustrate the points I want to make.

The first point is obvious—namely, that whatever policy may be chosen, it must inevitably represent, as those I have given as examples represent, an interference by the Government in the functioning of the whole economic and financial mechanism. That is the fundamental fact from which, in view of the very nature of the problem, there seems to be no escape. For the problem is how to render, not the individual, but the national economic system less susceptible to the bumps of this bumpy world.

Now an increase of Government intervention to protect the national economic system from the risks of depression will, in the first instance, lead to a growth of economic nationalism and isolation. It is obvious that it has done so, and it is inevitable that it should do so at first.

Depressions develop fast, Governments improvise measures, they experiment and are loath to wait to persuade others to experiment with them; they are restricted perhaps in different ways in the measures they dare take by political or constitutional considerations, or, equally important, by the state of public education on economic and financial questions. They are under pressure from those who believe that the depression had its origin abroad and can be warded off by keeping out foreign goods. The very nature of the measures currently employed, diversification of industry and agriculture, and the creation of collective demand imply some measure of isolation? Why not a full measure?

But the problem is a world problem. You cannot expect a depression to occur in one of the great industrial States without spreading far and wide. Immediately, the contraction of that country's demand will affect the price of raw materials and foodstuffs and hence all mining and agricultural countries. The reduction in the purchasing power of these producers of primary goods will affect all the other industrial countries which were in the habit of selling to them. It is a world problem that cannot be solved nationally. Efforts to isolate a national market must diminish the purchasing power of other countries, and thus the export industries of the self-isolating State. Large-scale Government expenditure or any other policy of credit expansion must influence the domestic price level and may create a disequilibrium between it and prices abroad. As such disequilibria arise, currencies are threatened, deflationary strains come into play, and so the trough of the depression moves from country to country and threatens those from which it has moved again with its backwash as one currency or another collapses.

Is it not as inevitable that the second phase of the growth of Government intervention in economic life should be the development of international co-operation, as that its first phase is the development of economic nationalism? As Governments become more and more conscious of their collective risks, accentuated by the three factors I have been considering, they will want to plan ahead. They will want to elaborate joint schemes to stimulate demand; they will want to synchronize their policies.

The first sign of the realization of this need by Governments has just made itself apparent in the discussions of the last Assembly at Geneva. It was there proposed by the Australian Delegation, and, after a number of other delegations had spoken in support, finally decided, that an examination should be made of the measures which might be employed with a view to the prevention or mitigation of economic depressions.

That resolution constitutes the formal recognition by the Governments of the League States that the problem of depressions is an international one and at least an implication that it is one demanding joint action and joint policies. It remains to be seen whether such policies can be elaborated before we find ourselves immersed in the next depression; whether, indeed, our knowledge of causes or of means of mitigation is yet sufficient to render the elaboration of a rational collective policy possible. But the simple fact that Governments have agreed that practical measures should be sought should be a stimulus to confidence. For, if they are sought and found, not only will the particular risks to which I have drawn attention be diminished, but out of the evil of depressions may emerge closer international collaboration and a better international understanding.

As I interpret recent history, then, the present widespread feeling of insecurity in the world is due largely to the working of certain profound economic forces, which do in fact accentuate collective economic risks. The first serious attempts by Governments to protect the economic structure have necessarily been empirical and have necessarily been conducted on a national scale. They have led to economic isolation. But that phase must pass, as it is more and more generally understood that the influence of those forces is world-wide. International co-operation must increase—not because one group of statesmen or another desires it—but simply because it is indispensable—because the risks in the stage of economic development that we have reached cannot be averted save by international consultation and concerted action.

II

THE DISTRIBUTION OF POWER AND LEADERSHIP

by Prof. J. B. Condliffe, D.Sc., M.A.

The subject of this lecture series is the world's economic future. I, for one, am not a prophet and cannot pretend to foretell even the immediate future. All that one can do is draw attention to significant trends of development in the recent past which seem likely to project themselves into the future. Even this limited objective presents a task in which past observers have not been conspicuously successful. It is not easy, among the complex and confused threads of economic activity, interwoven as they are with other elements of the social system, to distinguish those that set the pattern to-day, still less to say which are likely to persist and exert an important influence upon the pattern of the future. If I may change the metaphor, we may perhaps, by economic and historical analysis, discern the main outlines of the future, but only "as in a glass darkly." The analytic mirror we use may be faulty or our vision defective, so that the outline is blurred and may be quite distorted. Adam Smith, writing as the Industrial Revolution of the eighteenth century was gathering way, did not seem to have a very clear vision of the mechanical age that lay ahead of him.

The classical economists, arguing for Free Trade
a hundred years ago, committed themselves to
predictions of agricultural security that were soon
to be falsified by the application of steam to shipping
and railway transport and by refrigeration.[1] How
much more hazardous must economic prediction be
in this age when the pace of discovery has so
quickened in the natural sciences. Our own generation has seen a revolution in applied chemistry. The
production of natural dyes and fertilizers has been
largely displaced by that of synthetic products. Rayon
has shaken the market for silk. Wood-pulp has
changed the paper-making industry. At the moment
there is the most strenuous search for new synthetic
products to replace natural textile fibres as well as
rubber and petrol, and the chemists may soon produce
detergent fats from mineral oils in sufficient quantity

[1] "No country is likely to send any stock to England or, indeed, has
any to send, with the exception of the countries round Hamburgh, and
the imports thence cannot be considerable. In the Ukraine and other
countries in the South of Russia there is a remarkably fine breed of cattle ;
but then it is impossible to import them alive into England or otherwise
than salted, and as already seen, our merchants have enjoyed the privilege of doing this for a series of years, under a moderate duty, without
so much as a cwt. of beef having all the while been brought from Odessa
or the sea of Azof.

"The same is the case with South America : no live cattle can be sent
from it ; and no salt beef has ever come from it under the 12/–, nor will
an ounce ever come under the 8/– duty, or indeed though there were no
duty at all. The South Americans rarely if ever send beef to the West
Indies and how then is it to be supposed they should send it to England ?"

"Memorandum on the Proposed Importation of Foreign Beef and
Live Stock," by J. R. McCulloch, 1842, quoted in L. C. A. Knowles'
*The Industrial and Commercial Revolutions in Great Britain During the
Nineteenth Century*, London, 1921.

to disturb the vegetable and animal fat industries. Physics has contributed electrical power and revolutionized means of communication, and no one can foresee what new sources of energy may be developed. Biology may have even greater surprises in store for us.

Nor is the probable progress of applied science the only unknown in our equation. We must also reckon with political factors. There is, first of all, the possibility of destructive war with all its aftermath of disillusion and economic distortion. Hardly less serious are the possibilities of national fears and animosities twisting and cramping the free development of the world's resources by international specialization and co-operation. Who can foretell the drift of national economic policies? Will Government intervention continue to increase as in recent years or will there come a reaction towards greater individual liberty?

In his opening lecture Mr. Loveday has drawn attention to certain changes in the structure of industry and trade that seem likely to result from the stabilizing of population in the Western world and from the increase of mechanical methods of production. The economic world that he foresees is a bumpier world. My task to-night is to survey briefly the movements of population, of industrial development, and of commerce in different areas in order to discover how far and whither the balance of economic power and leadership seems to be shifting.

There is a sense in which the answer to this question lies outside the realm of economic observation and analysis. It must perhaps be sought in a more profound analysis of our changing civilization. In a much-quoted passage written just after the close of the last great war, General Smuts expressed his belief that great changes were imminent in our civilization.

"There is no doubt," he wrote, "that Mankind is once more on the move. The very foundations have been shaken and loosened, and things are again fluid. The tents have been struck and the great caravan of Humanity is once more on the march."[1]

We are all aware that in the twenty years since these lines were written immense forces of social change have been at work. It has proved impossible to confine these forces within the institutional framework that was reconstructed on the pre-war model. Apart from the ferment set in action by the revolution in Russia, there has been a general unsettlement of social ideas. Economic reconstruction broke down in an unparalleled depression which itself promoted the spread of new economic doctrines. We are still in the throes of post-war political changes, national and international. These are visible—perhaps superficial—evidences of changing ideas. In religious ideas and in social attitudes—for example, towards such basic institutions as the family, and in the assertion of the right to subsistence, as well as in

[1] J. C. Smuts, *The League of Nations: A Practical Suggestion*, London, 1918.

the progress towards economic equality—there is a degree of change so great as to be subversive of existing institutions. The economic future must be greatly influenced by such fundamental developments in social attitudes and beliefs. The effect of tendencious education can be very marked within a generation. The loosening of traditional sanctions is equally potent.

Economic organization is only one, and perhaps not the most important aspect of a civilization. It is perfectly true that "a civilization does not consist in machine-sewing or rifle-shooting or tea- and coffee- and cocoa-drinking or tobacco-smoking."[1] Nevertheless, the economic activity which provides a more abundant standard of life provides also the material basis for leisure, scholarship, and the arts— to say nothing of their patronage. The movement towards economic equality which in our generation is spreading an appreciation of the things of the spirit and liberating creative possibilities among the masses of the people, depends largely upon a higher level of economic production. It is, no doubt, important to distinguish between accumulation and culture, but there is too much specious talk about a necessary antithesis between material and spiritual development. In the past the two have mostly gone together, but have been the privilege of a small class. Given the trend to economic equality they are to-day more closely linked—material prosperity depending upon widespread cultural development and providing the

[1] A. J. Toynbee, *A Study of History*, vol. i, p. 429, Oxford, 1934.

opportunity for further development, not of a few only but of the whole society.

I do not feel it necessary, therefore, to apologize for confining my attention to a survey of economic tendencies. I take it for granted that scientific progress will continue and be accelerated, that the mechanical age in which we live will become more mechanical and so free an increasing number of individuals from the pressure of poverty and obsession with material needs. Whether they will use their freedom to cultivate the things of the spirit is primarily a problem of social education, perhaps the greatest problem with which our age is confronted.

In the past the centre of economic gravity has shifted along the lines of communication, and, in modern times, always westward, from Egypt to Greece and Rome, later to the Italian city-states, over the Alpine passes to the south-German river-cities, and thence to Portugal, Spain, Holland, France, and to England. The shift, however, has never been predetermined by purely economic considerations and there have always been competing possibilities. New means of transport opening up wider trade areas and the possession of material resources upon which developing economic activity could be based were clearly important; but national and international political considerations, based ultimately upon complex social forces, were even more important at many turning-points of history. Consider the decline of Spain after it had built up the first great Western empire. Or the exhausting effects of the wars between the petty states of Germany. Perhaps the most interesting illustration of the interaction of political factors, however, is provided by the wresting of economic leadership from France by Great Britain at the beginning of the nineteenth century. Leaving on one side the weaknesses of the French social organization, it is clear that Britain's economic development was made possible not only by rich coal deposits and by trading enterprise, but also by the long prior period of domestic peace, political adaptation, and detachment from the troubled politics of continental Europe. It has been said that the cultivation of the turnip pulled England through the Napoleonic wars, but the new farming of which the turnip was the symbol depended upon political and legal as well as economic adaptation.[1]

In the nineteenth century Britain followed up its advantage not only by the development of a great empire, but also by the creation of a virtually worldwide economic system based upon trade and investment. It is not always realized how much the international economic organization of the pre-war period was centred on, and directed from, London. The so-called gold standard was, in fact, a sterling standard. Britain was the entrepôt for the world's trade, and the London Money Market was its financial reservoir. Free trade, shipping, and railways built with British capital in all the continents were among the principal means of this expansion of British enterprise. But this system is ended. Its great

[1] Cf. L. C. A. Knowles, op. cit., pp. 364–6.

achievements in the sphere of foreign investment and monetary stability have been gravely impaired. Free trade has been abandoned. The rapid increase of population that spread from these islands to the colonies of settlement and contributed largely to the growth of the United States is slowing up.

I do not for a moment suggest that the political and economic power of the British Commonwealth has passed its peak and is now bound to decline. It would be silly to under-estimate the enormous strength of Great Britain's international position. In command over foodstuffs and raw material resources, in the vitality of its people at home and in the dominions, in the accumulated experience and established organization of its far-flung political, economic, and financial connections, Great Britain possesses reserves of power that the whole world recognizes. Nor can it be argued from the experience of a generation that has suffered from the crippling costs of a great war and the loss of a large proportion of its potential leadership, that the spirit of enterprise has given place to passivity.

Nevertheless, it seems clear that if the broken international mechanism is to be restored, the task is one which must be undertaken by international co-operation. We cannot expect that Great Britain can re-create a world system like that which it led in the nineteenth century. The balance of economic power has altered while increasing efficiency of communication has knit the whole world into closer neighbourhood. It is, I believe, a sound political instinct that has led this country to work through the League of Nations on the one hand and strive for closer co-operation with the United States of America on the other. Whatever may be thought of the discouraging setbacks experienced at Geneva or of British policy therein, some means of international consultation and collaboration is now essential, and the League at present provides the best available mechanism. This is particularly true of the routine but vitally important processes of technical collaboration which tend to be obscured by the limelight thrown upon political discussions at Geneva. In an increasing number of matters of common concern, the whole world has become a close neighbourhood. Public health, preventive medicine, nutrition, and transport may be cited as fields where common action by governments is conspicuously necessary. The experience of recent years provides ample proof that only by co-ordinated international action can effective measures be taken to reconstruct the broken trading, financial, and monetary mechanisms of the world.

When one surveys the recent trends of economic development this conviction is reinforced. If these trends could be summed up in one sentence, it would be that the relative weight of Europe in world production and world trade shows signs of declining. The growing parts of the world are the more distant countries. It is not only a matter of population, but of raw material resources and of developing industries. The new world, moreover, is less troubled

with the feuds and vendettas that have turned
Europe again into an armed camp, and it has been
less harassed by the paraphernalia of the new protectionism which is the economic counterpart of
rearmament. It is difficult to resist the conviction
that we are witnessing the gradual development of
a new economic system, necessarily international in
character, in which the centre of gravity is again
moving westward. Mr. Loveday has drawn attention
to the manner in which the slowing up of population
increase in western Europe and the trend to indirect
methods of production are tending to promote the
industrial development of the newer countries. It is
true that their populations also are tending towards
a stabilizing of numbers, but there will be a lag of
perhaps a generation since their people, reinforced
until recently by immigrants in the prime of life,
are younger on the average. In the next generation
the economic importance not only of the United
States but of the British dominions and of the South
American countries must surely continue to increase.

For much the same reason it is probable that we
must expect a growth of industrial manufacture in
the hitherto backward countries of eastern and
central Europe. A glance at the population map of
Europe shows that numbers are still increasing fast
in a great belt of country from Poland to Greece.
Part of this increase is obviously due to the stoppage
of trans-Atlantic emigration. Some of it also is due
to the closing of western European countries to
immigrants in the years since the depression. Birth

rates are beginning to decline but are still high in eastern Europe, while death rates are falling with the introduction of modern hygiene and industrial development fostered by the new spirit of nationalism has already made rapid strides.[1]

If we look further ahead we must probably reckon with the beginnings of a new cycle of population increase in the great peasant masses of the Far East. In Japan the cycle is already well developed with economic and political consequences that need no elaboration.[2] In Soviet Russia there has been a forced industrialization accompanied by a rapid population increase and a complete reorganization of agriculture. India's population is rapidly approaching the 400 million mark, and students of Chinese population agree that some increase of numbers has begun in that country also. The stirring of new life in these great peasant masses may prove to be one of the most significant developments of our time. Will it turn towards the new forms of economic organization pioneered in Soviet Russia? Or can Western capitalism re-create an international trading and investment system that will provide the means for reconstruction of these Far Eastern civilizations? Or will Japan develop her industrial leadership into a hegemony of Asia?

This question has direct bearing upon the argument developed last week by Mr. Loveday con-

[1] League of Nations, *World Economic Survey*, 1931–2.
[2] E. F. Penrose, *Population Theories and Their Application*, Stanford, 1934.

cerning the probable fall in demand for elementary necessities as a result of the stabilizing of population in western Europe and the Western world generally. It is obvious that these great peasant masses of Asia offer a potential market greatly in need of more abundant food supplies, of clothing, boots and shoes, and rudimentary necessities. They lack the means with which to procure such things, and before they can develop extra production to provide purchasing power they must somewhere get not only capital but help in reorganizing their political and social structure. Must we admit that our Western civilization is incapable of giving them this help? The development of such markets would be a boon to the older industrial countries. In the nineteenth century British capital and enterprise did in fact prove capable of such initiative in many areas. The great advances in the standard of living which marked that century were the direct result of opening out new markets and developing new resources. Is it impossible to devise means of international collaboration whereby the industrial creditor countries can effectively aid China and in so doing help to solve their own production problems? Or must China turn for help to the methods of Soviet Russia? Or will Japan take up the "white man's burden" in the Far East? The answer to these questions, I suggest, will provide one of the main clues to the solution of the conundrum which has been posed to the lecturers in this series.

If we turn from population to consider the distribution of raw materials and the industrial structure that has been built upon them, we can see the same tendency towards more rapid growth in the newer countries. Professor Högbom has pointed out that the earth's crust does not contain pure mineral ores, but may be likened to a slag-heap containing mixed traces of minerals remaining after a great furnace has cooled down.[1] For centuries Europeans have been scratching round in their corner of this slag-heap. They are still fortunate enough to possess ample quantities of coal and iron, the basic materials of industry; but as industry develops and needs new alloys and new materials, there is a persistent tendency towards the opening up and exploration of new areas. The United States and Russia are very rich in mineral resources and therefore enjoy a substantial advantage in industrial production, an advantage that is more likely to increase than decrease as time goes on. It suffices to recall the recent development of copper in the Belgian Congo and Rhodesia, and of tin in Malaya and Bolivia, to demonstrate how vital access to new sources of raw materials has proved to the great industrial and trading countries. The current controversy concerning access to raw materials reflects the anxiety of those countries which have failed to secure or to hold colonial areas upon which they can rely for future supplies. The extraordinary development in recent years of international cartel and control schemes in the mineral industries is perhaps signifi-

[1] Ivar Högbom, *Mineral Production.*

cant of the necessity that Mr. Loveday argued for new methods of international co-operation to develop out of the present phase of economic nationalism.[1]

At this point I should like to draw attention to a calculation recently made by the economic Intelligence Service of the League of Nations. In order to compile an index of world manufacturing production it became necessary to calculate the relative value of such production in the leading industrial countries. Data were available for 23 countries which between them account for well over 90 per cent of the total value added to raw materials in the process of manufacturing in the world as a whole. The estimate finally arrived at was that the United States alone was responsible for 45 per cent of the total value of manufacturing production. Next in order came Germany 12, Great Britain 10, France 8, Soviet Russia 5, Italy 3·4, Japan 2·6, Canada 2·5, and Belgium 2.[2] The United States manufactured a greater total value than the whole of industrial Europe combined if Soviet Russia is excluded.

It seems obvious that, with a population relatively more concentrated in the younger age-groups and therefore still increasing faster than in western Europe, with enormous reserves of minerals and the largest area of free trade and specialization the world has ever known, the economic power of the

[1] W. Y. Elliott and others, *International Control in the Non-Ferrous Metals*, New York, 1937.

[2] League of Nations, *World Production and Prices*, 1935–6, Geneva, 1936.

United States is likely to increase. It is important to stress the fact that the great free-trade area makes possible the development of specialization, large-scale marketing, and mass-production methods in regard to the articles of durable consumption and capital equipment towards which demand turns more and more. It is no accident that the United States dominates the production of such commodities as automobiles, radios, and refrigerators, and is pioneering such inventions as air-conditioning on railway trains.

Industrial development is proceeding apace also in countries that have hitherto concentrated mainly on agriculture. Not only in eastern Europe and in Soviet Russia, but in Brazil and the Argentine, in the British dominions, in Japan, and to some extent in countries like China, India, and the Netherlands Indies there is rapid progress in the simpler manufactures.[1] This progress has clearly been hastened by

[1] The following table shows the rapid development of industrial production in several of the newer industrial countries for which indices are available. Comparable indices are not available for many countries in which there has been similar development, e.g. Argentine, Brazil, Australia, New Zealand. In reading this table allowance must be made for rearmament activity in several countries.

INDICES OF INDUSTRIAL PRODUCTION, 1936

(*Base*: 1929 = 100)

				1932	1936
U.S.S.R.	...	...	...	183	382
Japan ...	...	...	...	98	151
Latvia ...	...	...	...	82	143
Greece ...	...	...	...	101	139

(*Continued on next page*)

the gradual closing of markets in industrial Europe for the export-surpluses of the specialized agricultural countries. It is perhaps true that the prospect of stable and older populations in industrial Europe

(Continued from previous page)

Finland ...	...	...	...	83	133
Denmark	...	...	...	91	130
Roumania	...	...	...	89	130
Hungary	...	...	...	77	129
Sweden ...	...	...	...	—	129
Chile	...	...	...	87	124
Estonia ...	...	...	...	78	120
United Kingdom		...	...	84	116
Norway	...	...	...	100	115
Germany	...	...	...	53	106
Canada ...	...	...	...	58	90
U.S.A. ...	...	...	...	54	88
Italy	...	...	...	67	88
Belgium	...	...	...	69	87
Austria ...	...	...	...	60	81
Czechoslovakia ...		...	...	64	80
Poland ...	...	...	...	54	72
Netherlands	...	...	...	62	72
France ...	...	...	...	69	70

The development is even clearer in the case of textile production.

INDICES OF TEXTILE PRODUCTION

(Base: 1929 = 100)

					1932	1936
Chile	...	...	...		284	227
Latvia	...	...	...		109	201
Greece	...	...	...		120	179
Roumania	...	...	...		129	157
Denmark	...	...	...		112	147
Austria ...	...	...	...		87	146
Finland ...	...	...	...		89	144

(Continued on next page)

has encouraged the attempts to protect their agriculture, but it is also true that much of the agricultural protection of recent years has had political rather than economic purposes. Agriculture is regarded as a bulwark of the existing social order and for this domestic reason as well as in the effort to increase self-sufficiency of food supplies in the event of war, agriculture has been given preferential treatment. The inevitable result has been that the agricultural countries have reinforced their industrial protection so that the new economic system which is developing tends to pass out of the European orbit.

The United States is strategically placed to take advantage of these developments. She has the inside track with Canada in the north and the rapidly developing countries of Latin America in the south. Across the Pacific she faces the awakening masses of Asia as well as the British dominions of Australia and New Zealand. Yet she retains close connections across the Atlantic with Europe.

It is common knowledge that both domestic and

(*Continued from previous page*)

Hungary	...	...	...	94	142
Japan ...	...	...	...	105	135
Canada ...	...	...	...	75	123
Germany	...	...	...	87	107
United Kingdom		...	...	86	104
U.S.A. ...	...	...	...	72	97
Czechoslovakia ...		...	...	68	91
Belgium	...	...	...	64	81
Poland ...	...	...	...	63	80
France ...	...	...	...	65	73
Italy ...	...	...	...	66	69

international economic developments have forced
and are forcing the United States to a reconsidera-
tion of her external economic relations. Within her
borders the frontier has disappeared and there has
actually been a reflux of population from the poorer
agricultural areas. The financial effect of the war
was to change her status from that of a debtor nation
to that of the largest creditor country. Her shipping
has rapidly increased and her trading advantage,
combined with her isolation from the troubled politics
of Europe, has resulted in an unprecedented accumulation of gold reserves, the ultimate symbol of
financial power. By a great act of statesmanship her
far-sighted Secretary of State has reversed her traditional tariff policy so as to adapt her trade to the
necessities of her new international situations. It is
perhaps not yet sufficiently realized that this break
with long-cherished tradition is of first-rate historical
importance.

It must surely be evident that no effective international organization is now possible without the
co-operation if not the leadership of the United
States. We seem to me to be in a painful period of
transition when international co-operation is more
necessary than ever, but beyond the single-handed
powers of any one nation. The pre-war international
system has broken down and cannot be restored.
Reconstruction of a new system demands concerted
effort, but the nation whose power is greatest and
seems likely to be greater still, is still too preoccupied
with its own domestic problems to play the leading

rôle for which it is cast. I do not subscribe to the view that because alien immigration has temporarily swamped the Anglo-Saxon elements of the American population this must necessarily result in a lowering of economic efficiency or of cultural standards. It is true that the assimilation of diverse racial and cultural groups is a long, difficult, and in many respects a painful process. At the moment also the United States is going through a veritable social revolution, the outcome of which is difficult to foresee. The frontier age has gone and with it the "rugged individualism" so long characteristic of the American system. The country has been launched upon a series of legislative experiments involving centralization and government intervention suddenly and without time to devise the necessary administrative mechanism such as a highly efficient civil service. In the same way it has not yet developed the financial or diplomatic mechanisms consonant with its new international position. Ultimately a vigorous and rich culture may develop out of the merging of such diverse racial elements; but I hope it may not seem too cynical to suggest that the passing of economic power to the United States reinforces Mr. Loveday's prediction that the world's economic future is likely to be a bumpy one.

There is little need to emphasize the bumpiness of the outlook in Europe. Apart from the highly dangerous economic policies that have been and are being followed by the dictatorship countries, Europe is paying a heavy price for its political feuds. I do not pretend to be able to estimate how long a country like Germany can afford to pursue at such heavy cost her policies of self-sufficiency and economic regimentation, nor how far the cost of Italy's imperialist adventures has impaired her economic efficiency. There are ample evidences of economic strain in these countries however they may be camouflaged by financial virtuosity. From the point of view of my subject here, however, I am more concerned with the effect of political unsettlement upon the commercial organization of the European countries. The share of Europe in world trade has steadily declined since 1932, but, in fact, the decline is concentrated in the trade of those countries where exchange control has been extended into an ingenious system designed to direct trade as an instrument of national policy. Torn by political rivalries, their economic life distorted by a confusion of restrictive trade devices, burdened by very heavy armaments, the European countries run grave risks of losing still more ground to the developing new countries.

There are, however, two other possibilities in the present situation to which attention should be drawn. A generation hence it seems probable that we shall look back upon the years just behind us as the period of another great debasement of the world's currencies. Debasement in modern times does not take the crude form of putting into circulation coins of lower intrinsic value, but the wholesale depreciation of currencies, creation of cheap credit, and finally enlargement of the gold reserves upon which new credit may be based is even more effective. We may find that the consequences of cheap credit are more far-reaching in the long run than the immediate purposes for which it was created. If history is any guide we may find ourselves, provided we can escape the cataclysm of another great war, passing through another fairly long period of rising prices. In such periods the real burden of past debts is reduced and a premium is given to enterprise as against property. When the monetary yardsticks are altered in this way, great social changes are induced since the revaluation of goods and services is very uneven and affects human rewards as well as the prices of commodities. One of the effects of rising prices in the past has been to stimulate the development of new resources in the overseas countries, and this consideration quite clearly reinforces the tendencies sketched earlier in this lecture.

In the long run, however, power and leadership in the economic as in any other field of human endeavour depend less upon circumstances than upon men, and less upon numbers than upon quality. The essential problem confronting this or any other country in its effort to raise and make more secure the standard of life of its people is the development and training of men and women capable of grappling with changing circumstances. In the difficult period through which we are passing it is the country which most successfully enlists capacity wherever it is found which stands the best chance of survival. Leadership is more necessary than ever, but it must be leadership based upon and drawn from an educated and stable democracy. The day has gone by when a privileged caste can command the acquiescent following of ignorant masses with any hope of final success. The problems with which we are confronted are problems of adaptation to a rapidly changing world.

> "We sail a changeful sea through halcyon days and storm,
> And when the ship laboureth, our stedfast purpose
> Trembles like as the compass in a binnacle.
> Our stability is but balance, and wisdom lies
> in masterful administration of the unforeseen."

It is not by clinging to past privileges or by attempting to retain and protect group interests threatened by their failure to keep pace with the times, but by shrewd adaptation and foresight that economic leadership is won. It cannot be kept in cold storage but must continually be rewon. Such a task demands that a nation must use all its capacity. A greater measure of economic equality, improved nutrition, and physical fitness are all elements of the problem, but educational opportunity is at least equally important, opportunity not so much to acquire knowledge, though knowledge is important, but for mental training and social understanding. Economic power will fall as it always has in the past to the nation that knows best how to discover and train its potential leaders, "building them fair and fronting to the dawn."

III

ON THE FUTURE ECONOMIC ORGANIZATION OF SOCIETY

by B. OHLIN

WHY do we attempt to form opinions about the future? Is it anything but a childish curiosity which leads us to undertake this hopeless task? Personally, I think it is something more than that. We are all of us forced to act with the future in mind, for our actions are concerned with the future. Every business man, every politician, indeed every human being, is on many occasions forced to form an opinion about a future situation before deciding which course to follow. Some people say that economists have to prophesy; I think, on the contrary, that economists, almost alone of all those who have to deal with economic matters, are able, if they wish to, to confine themselves to a study of what has already happened. Indeed, it is wise, when undertaking scientific studies, to do so. To-day I shall, however, make an exception, as I have been asked to do, and shall speculate a little about some future economic tendencies.

The speakers who have preceded me have dealt with several important problems. I shall attempt to discuss some correlated questions which concern the *organization of society* with special reference to economic activity.

E

In every such inquiry it is probably wise to begin with some observations about the tendencies which have characterized the last decades. If there are no special reasons for expecting a change, one can assume a certain probability of a further movement in the same direction. Hence, one has to establish what this direction has been, and then to analyse carefully all possible reasons for a change in movement.

In my opinion, the chief characteristic of change in the organization of society in the last half-century has been the *growth of central organization and control.* Trusts and cartels have increased in number and importance. Some of them have been created entirely on private initiative, others have been fostered by public measures. Looser industrial and branch associations also attract growing interest and acquire a rising influence. Furthermore, municipal and government enterprise now covers a much wider field, and government supervision also reaches many kinds of private economic activity. If we turn to that kind of business which is yet, on the whole, in private hands without any public control or monopolistic organization, we find a tendency for large-scale enterprise to grow, particularly as far as the financial control is concerned. This is also a kind of central organization.

The discussion of this problem in recent years has often been rather confused. We have talked as if the real issue was *to plan or not to plan,* and people have taken sides for or against planning. But as I understand it, this is not the real issue at all. Planning is necessary if we are to act, because, as already indicated, all our actions refer to the future; in fact, the business man who fails to plan will not remain long in business. The real issue, therefore, seems to me to be: *Are we to have more central control or less?* Are decisions to be more centralized than to-day, or will there be a reversion towards decentralization? Which forms of central control are needed? What rôle will political institutions play in management and control?

These questions are naturally difficult to answer. One has to consider what is useful as well as what is probable. Two observations, however, can be made with safety. Firstly it is improbable that a form of organization which is practical and useful in one field will fit all other spheres of economic activity also. On the contrary, we must expect that, if we are to achieve favourable results, many different types of organization will have to be used in different fields. Secondly, the problem is much wider than the mere question of what rôle state and municipal institutions are to play, the extent of their enterprise and controlling activity. It is just as much a question of the importance of giant enterprises, trusts, cartels, and other forms of private organization.

As already indicated, the last decades have been characterized by a growth of central organization of many different kinds. Has this been a mistake? Would it have been better to have retained the old forms of organization of a looser, more decentralized kind? Or have the changes corresponded to actual needs? In discussing such questions we must, of course, apply commonly accepted standards of value, e.g. the desirability of a high and secure standard of life. Some are inclined to answer the last of these questions in the negative. They refer to the freer organization of the nineteenth century, and point out that it functioned fairly well. That is true, but does it justify the conclusion that it ought to have been retained? To form an opinion on this question it is necessary to ask why the relatively loose liberal organization of last century could function; we will then see to what extent the same circumstances exist to-day, and whether it is probable that a similar organization would be practical under present conditions or not.

Let me begin by mentioning a few outstanding features which seem to me to explain why a loose system could work fairly well a hundred years ago. The nineteenth century was an expanding economic universe. Technical progress was very rapid, and population was growing at a pace which the world had almost certainly never seen before. New areas were opened up for agriculture and raw material production and later on for manufacturing industries. International capital movements were enormously bigger than ever before, and helped to bring about a rapid expansion in the new countries. If the productive apparatus had become too large in a certain industry, one had but to wait a few years for the actual need to catch up with productive capacity. Thus an actual reduction of that capacity was seldom necessary, and cartels or other agreements to bring about its reduction were more or less superfluous.

Fixed capital played but a small rôle in industry and transportation at that time. Hence production could be adapted much more easily to all kinds of changes than is now the case. Furthermore, the productive units were smaller and that also, on the whole, gave them a greater ability to adapt themselves to a changing world.

An exceedingly important factor was the freedom of international migration. The United States and other transoceanic areas were open for immigration from Europe. Hence, European manufacturing nations felt much less need of unemployment relief and other kinds of social policy than they do to-day. One may say that emigration to some extent was an alternative to social policy and regulation of agriculture in Europe. Certainly this was the case in the last two or three decades of the nineteenth century.

One could perhaps mention as a separate factor that the price system functioned rather smoothly. The patterns of behaviour in business were individualistic, partly for the reasons given above and partly, I think, for psychological reasons. Hence, there was less need of government interference with pricing than has been the case more recently.

Let us turn now to *the post-war situation*. Obviously, conditions have been rather different, and it is only natural that they have called forth a different organization. For instance, technical development has increased the economies and other advantages of large-scale production; larger technical units, therefore, and above all larger financial units have grown up. Furthermore, fixed costs play to-day a much greater rôle than they did some decades ago, and this fact has been a factor in changing the conditions and rules of competition. "Perfect competition" is becoming less and less important (it never was so dominant as economists believed) and a development of something which is often called "monopolistic competition" is taking its place.

A second and not less important factor is the growth of organizations on the labour market. While labour unions are no doubt necessary to help the workers in what would otherwise be a very unfavourable position in their negotiations with the employers, it is obvious that the result of organizations among workers and employers is to make wages a rather "sticky" cost element. Hence, costs of production adapt themselves less easily, at least downwards, than was formerly the case. Here again the flexibility seems to have been much smaller than was generally assumed before the war, but there can be no doubt that the adaptability has declined. A third factor is the reduction in the international mobility of labour. Emigration is no longer a substitute for an economic and social policy which alleviates distress and reduces unemployment.

One may, perhaps, add that the economic depressions of the last twenty years have been more serious than those of the forty years preceding the war; and one may also justifiably stress that the present monetary system is less automatic than the pre-war gold standard. As one piece of relatively automatic machinery breaks down so it becomes necessary more completely than before to manage also the rest of the system. Thus, managed currency, controlled international migration, and a controlled wage level make the whole system less able to adapt itself to changing conditions without conscious control over a wide area and in many different respects. One may say, in fact, that fundamental economic changes have increased the need for organization, or rather for a more central direction of economic life. This direction is handled partly by public institutions, but to a large extent also by private business organizations.

The most obvious example of a case where management is necessary to prevent serious misfortune is that of a major depression. When prices begin to fall, it is to the advantage of each individual firm to buy as little as possible. This tends to intensify the crisis. Thus, it is obvious that the automatic reaction of the individual firm does not in this case lead to a re-establishment of balance. On the contrary, there are certain "self-inflammatory" tendencies in the economic system which will spread if they are not consciously counteracted. Such action assumes either agreement between a large number of business men or intervention by public institutions.

What I have said so far concerns *the greater need for organization* to-day compared with fifty years ago. This, however, is only one aspect of the process which has led to a society of our present type. The other aspect is *our growing ability to organize*. Systems of communication like the telegraph, telephone, and radio, and such mechanical tools as typewriters and calculating machines, make it much more easy than formerly to handle large-scale organizations effectively. *Pari passu* with this development of certain mechanical tools has gone an improvement in the methods of large-scale management. Office technique and book-keeping have adapted themselves to the conditions of giant firms, concerns, and associations; statistical methods have been developed and the experience of managers has grown. We have, in fact, a much greater ability to handle large units than we had half a century ago.

For anyone who turns his attention to all these factors it ceases to be surprising that the organization of society has been subject to a radical change and that organizations have come to play a much more important rôle than formerly. Obviously, one cannot say that this development is arbitrary. On the contrary, it must be regarded chiefly as a practical adaptation of human methods to actual needs.

So far in this account I have neglected one aspect which many people regard as the most important of all. Contemporaneously with the technical and economic changes has come a slow but none the less radical change in *the attitude and mentality of business men*. There is much more of a will to co-operate to-day than fifty years ago. In my opinion, this has something to do with what one could call "the decline of optimism." People do not believe, as they used to do, that economic progress will continue indefinitely with only slight interruptions. Hence, they are no longer content to allow things to take their own course, but ask instead what they can do to guarantee that conditions in their own sphere improve or remain reasonable, giving a decent standard of living to the workers and fair profit to enterprise. One could perhaps say that the merchant mentality and the nineteenth-century belief in free competition have given way in our century to an engineer's mentality and a predilection for co-operation.

The pessimism which is one of the factors which explain this new mentality naturally leads to a claim not only for private organization but also for a social and economic policy by public institutions. Society must intervene, it is said, to reduce the insecurity under which we are living. This, I think, is the main basis for the far-reaching social insurance and un-employment policy which has developed in the last decades. It is no longer regarded as a concern only of the individual himself, if he suffers from unem-ployment, sickness, or invalidity; on the contrary, it is considered the duty of the community to come to his aid. He has a *right* to assistance, and need not appear as a beggar.

All these fundamental changes in economic con-ditions and in mental attitude would, however, not have led to the expansion of social policy which we have witnessed, if the continued economic progress had not *increased the resources* of the State and the municipalities. Only thereby has it become possible for the community to finance costly social measures.

The impression one gains from a review of the kind I have attempted to make is that the change in organization of our society in the last half-century can be regarded as a double adaptation to new technical and international conditions and to variations in the social outlook of man. There is, of course, a mutual interdependence between the new forms of organizations and the attitude and outlook which has led to them. The changed *milieu* and the changed psychology are parts of the same process, and it is largely arbitrary which one wishes to regard as cause and which one wishes to regard as effect.

That there is a certain inherent necessity in this development can hardly be doubted. Many people regard the interventionism of our days as an entirely mistaken policy, due only to the stupidity of politicians, but for such an interpretation of history there is no foundation. On the other hand, it is far from me to suggest that everything that has happened *has* been for the good. If we use value standards on which I think we can all agree—for instance, that (other things equal) a higher standard of living is preferable to a lower standard—then it is obvious that in many cases the policy pursued has been mistaken. For instance, erroneous views that the reduction of the working time from 48 hours to 40 hours need not have any influence on the consumption standard of a people, have led to great difficulties in certain countries. But in spite of such mistakes and those which have been so conspicuous in international trade policy, the dominating impression is that the organization of society has adapted itself to new conditions. It is quite impossible, and would certainly not be desirable if it were possible, to return to the forms of society which existed in industrialized countries half a century ago.

This sketch of the tendencies in economic organization is concerned with the development up to the last depression. *Since 1930* these tendencies have been much intensified. It must be added, however, that they have also been to a large extent distorted, in the sense that organizations and interventions have been created as a result of what appears to be a short-sighted and mistaken view of actual conditions and problems. It is only natural that the world economic depression has led to an enormous expansion of government intervention and regulation of business. Besides, widespread unemployment has caused an enormous expansion of public works and numerous other government measures. On the whole, the sphere of public action in economic life has grown and the number and power of organizations among business men have increased. Unfortunately, the erroneous impression, which is always gaining ground during times of poor business conditions, that the world has a surplus of commodities over and above needs, has led to a number of exaggerated restriction schemes. Output and sales have been restricted either by private organizations exclusively or by them in collaboration with governments.

The crisis in world agriculture, which is something different from the industrial depression, although it started about the same time, has perhaps led to more regulation of economic activity in recent years than anything else. In the majority of countries the regulation of production and sales of foodstuffs and raw materials for food is much more detailed than in the case of other products. Naturally, the desire for increased home production of foodstuffs and all kinds of raw materials as a precaution in case of war, had also contributed to measures of this kind. The war scare is indeed one of the chief causes of the growth of protectionism and autarchy in the last few years. The most obvious example of this is, of course, in Germany where General Göring's general staff for the four-year plan has taken over control of industry as a whole in an effort to build up facilities for the production within Germany of all necessary raw materials.

FUTURE DEVELOPMENT

The question which I am to try to answer here is, above all, whether these tendencies towards a more highly organized society are likely to continue or not. To form an opinion on this question it is necessary first of all to remember that many of the basic circumstances which have hitherto led to growth of organization remain. It seems fairly obvious that they will in the future also—at least for a decade or two—call for central direction and control in many ways. Migration between countries is as restricted as ever. The mentality which calls for security and collaboration has certainly not been weakened. The risk of depressions remains, and the public is much more aware of it than before the war. The restoration of a semi-automatic international monetary system like the pre-war gold standard looks a long way off. And the fear of war has perhaps never before been so pronounced as it is to-day.

It is more debatable whether the fundamental technical circumstances remain of a character that will call for a further growth of large-scale production and financial organization. On the one hand, it is obvious that in certain fields the growth of large-scale enterprise continues, e.g. railway companies are amalgamated and larger networks of electrification are created. Furthermore, the system of taxation in most countries seems to discourage the creation of new firms for the utilization of inventions or other kinds of initiative. If a new line of production is exploited by an existing large concern and leads to a loss, then this loss will be deducted from the profits of the concern, with a consequent reduction in taxes paid. Thus the State will carry its share of the risk of the new enterprise, just as it will take a share of the profits if the attempt succeeds and leads to large earnings. On the other hand, if production is taken up by a new company and it leads to a loss, the shareholders will carry the whole of this burden; whereas if profits result the State will take a part of them. It is easy to understand why, for instance, in the mechanical industry existing large concerns tend to spread themselves over a wider and wider field of activity.

On the other hand, it seems to be easier now than it was a decade or two ago for small technical units to work rather effectively in some industries. One important factor in this direction is the development of automatic machinery of a smaller size than could previously be obtained. The production of small but economical electric motors has also tended to reduce the costs of small firms, compared with those of large-scale enterprise. The motor lorry has reduced the costs of transportation for small firms relatively more than for large-scale enterprise, which could more easily be located close to a railway line with a siding of its own.

Statistics reveal that in several countries the number of small firms with five to ten workers has been growing rapidly since the war. Their growth seems to be even quicker than that of the giant enterprises, whilst units of medium size do not show the same ratio of expansion. It would be easy, however, to draw mistaken conclusions from this fact. First of all, a very large percentage of these small firms are not manufacturers, but simply repair shops for motor cars, so that when studying tendencies for manufacturing industries in general these repair shops must be disregarded, being something quite special. Turning to the small manufacturing concerns it is observed that many of them make only a small number of parts (e.g. of machines), selling them to a larger concern which assembles its own parts together with those it has purchased. Standardization and greater accuracy in measurement have lead to the spreading of production of parts between many different firms. In an economic sense, however, it may be said that all such small firms, working almost exclusively for a large enterprise, are parts really of one large organization, even if they have a certain formal financial independence. This fact must be stressed, as it is often overlooked. A small manufacturer, producing nothing but certain special parts for use by a large tractor factory, has an entirely different (and less independent) position from that of a small manufacturer of agricultural tools fifty years ago.

It is therefore most uncertain whether one may speak of any tendency for small-scale independent enterprise to grow, looking at the problem from the point of view which is relevant to a discussion of the organization of society. If we consider not production but marketing, it is safe to say that large-scale economies and advantages seem to be growing. One may perhaps sum up the impressions gained from a study of recent tendencies by saying that, on the one hand, large-scale enterprise is growing in the old sense, while on the other hand an increase of small productive units is taking place, but that many of these small firms are dependent for their sales on large firms, which latter exist because of advantages from large-scale financing and marketing. But one thing seems certain: that to interpret recent developments simply as a movement back to the nineteenth-century type of small, entirely independent economic units, is unjustifiable. Nothing in technical development suggests a need for a general return to nineteenth-century organization, and nothing in that social outlook which calls for security and protection against risks leads to the conclusion that recent tendencies will be reversed.

But it is obvious that, particularly during the last depression, many mistakes were made, simply because politicians were forced to take a short view and institute emergency measures which in the long run have a very detrimental influence on conditions in the country concerned and elsewhere. Now that the depression is receded an urgent need for adaptation to more normal conditions has become obvious. As experience has demonstrated considerable disadvantages in business from a bureaucratic form of government, it seems not unlikely that an adaptation to a more flexible system will be forthcoming. This, of course, depends on whether economic conditions remain relatively favourable during the next decade. The outburst of a new and serious depression would probably tend to intensify a bureaucratic intervention as well as the exaggerated protectionist policy which was the direct outcome of the recent crisis. But under good general business conditions such systems will, on the contrary, almost certainly be modified. This may be true even in cases where the main motive is a wish for security in the event of war. For it can easily be shown as mistaken to rely as much as some countries do to-day on uneconomical production at home. In several commodities it would be much better to build up relatively large stocks for use during wars or other such emergencies.

It is obvious that optimists and pessimists will have different opinions as to the extent to which such adaptations as these can be expected in the near future. Whilst the speed of the process will probably depend on conditions which cannot now be foreseen, it seems to me probable that, if a general deflation of the price level is prevented, some such adaptation will come. I make an exception, however, for the countries which are ruled by dictators with seemingly little awareness of the economic issues in modern times.

If I should try to summarize my view of the organization that is needed under existing conditions and the conditions which may be expected in the future, then I should say: first, that we need a system which provides means for central direction and control, e.g. to mitigate depressions, to check abuses, to finance technical research on a large scale, to avoid labour conflicts, to reduce risks of violent price fluctuations for agricultural products and raw materials, and so on, and secondly, that this system must not be bureaucratic, as it will be if centralization is pursued beyond a certain point. For example, to bring the larger part of industry and trade under direct public management and control would, in my opinion, lead in a few years to decreased flexibility and less dynamic force than a freer economic system could provide. There are some who, objecting to this conclusion, point out that many large limited companies are now under the control of managers who themselves own only a small part of the shares, and who have no particular thought for the immediate interests of large masses of shareholders, considering rather the future of the enterprise for its own sake. It is therefore contended that such firms could just as easily be under State ownership with these managers as civil servants working in the public interest. Already most managers in large firms with high salaries do not work simply for increased income, but rather to make a success of their business. Could they not work just as well in a State enterprise? Personally I find it impossible to accept this view, for political ownership necessarily involves a political discussion and control of many things. Red tape is unavoidable, and managers would, moreover, have to consider the views of political parties and the risks of propaganda among an electorate which understands little or nothing of the particular kind of business. Furthermore, public enterprises are much more securely entrenched and are, therefore, in less need to preserve flexibility and adaptability than is private enterprise. It is my view that there is a need for public measures tending to increase the mobility of production and trade, rather than to reduce it, as widespread nationalization would. For example, certain forms of private monopoly need strict public supervision to prevent vested interests from becoming an obstacle to progress.

A special danger in the restrictionist mentality which developed during the last depression is that private organizations of the cartel type often exercise a restrictionistic influence on production and trade. It is an understandable policy from their own point of view, for it can in many cases increase revenue, at least in the short run; but the outcome for society as a whole from such a policy, if it is generally pursued, will be the incomplete utilization of productive resources and a slowing down of economic expansion. There is, therefore, a real need for co-ordinating the work of organizations in different industries and trades, so as to make it advisable for each of them to increase their output, without the risk that this output cannot be sold owing to restricted output by other organizations. It must be remembered that the supply of certain goods is the source of the demand for others. Thus, if a number of industries restrict their sales, others are almost compelled to do the same. But if none restrict, except in very special cases and temporarily, then all can expand their output and sell it. Hence, the maintenance of the dynamic character of industry in a society where private organizations are numerous has become one of the most urgent needs of our time. In many Northern and Western industrialized countries population will soon cease to grow, and one of the chief dynamic factors of the last century will then disappear. There is, therefore, all the more need for keeping other dynamic forces alive, and individual initiative is probably the most important of all. It is hard to say how this initiative can be fully utilized unless economic activity is organized in a more decentralized manner than a nationalized industry would permit. On the other hand, some co-ordination of the efforts of various types of economic organisms, public or private, trusts or cartels, or organizations of a looser character, will be needed if depressions and other serious maladjustments are to be avoided.

In brief, a system is needed which *combines flexibility with the possibility of centralized direction* in certain special respects. Town-planning is perhaps the best example of a flexible form of centralized control. Town-planning provides limits to the free actions of the individual, but so long as he respects the rules of the game, he can do what he will. In my opinion, the principles behind town-planning can well be rationalized and expanded to cover not only larger regions but the whole national economic policy of a state or even a group of states. Economic policy in the last decade or so has been much too conservative, principally employing methods which have been developed for the solution of other tasks in pre-war time. Rationalization experts have a fruitful field for their labour in improving the methods of economic and social policy.

If I am right in saying that there exists a need for something like this, then I think one may also expect that an actual movement in this direction will come. And, if the fear of war should cease to dominate the mind of men, questions of social organization will come to the fore and will be discussed in a less stereotyped fashion than the pre-war debate on liberalism and socialism or the post-war discussion of "planning." We will then, no doubt, proceed to a revision of much that is hastily improvised in present-day economic policy. I hope that it will then also be found useful to attempt some *international co-operation on problems of national organization*, for in many cases a country can use one of several alternative methods of economic policy to solve its own problems, and there is no reason why international considerations should not lead it to adopt the alternative which is least damaging to other countries. In agreeing to this, it can secure a guarantee that those other countries will act similarly for the benefit of all. This does not in the least assume that the individual nations surrender their aims and objectives when these should lead to measures which are detrimental to other countries. But one tries to make them as little detrimental as possible. Particularly in agriculture, it should be possible to achieve all that is important for food-importing countries with much less damage to themselves and the exporting countries than that caused by present systems.

I make no prophecy about the extent of such changes in the economic organization of society. I confine myself to the statement that the problems concerned will become urgent in the next decade. Let us hope that they will be tackled with a little of the same energy and determination as that which the world is to-day applying to problems of war. If this is done and peace is preserved, then our economic future looks to me still promising. We can then, at least in Western Europe and North America, rapidly approach the goal which is within the sight of mankind for the first time in its history: the elimination of poverty.

IV

RECENT TENDENCIES IN ECONOMIC LIFE

by PROFESSOR E. F. HECKSCHER

THERE is only one thing certain with regard to the future, and that is its *un*certainty. This negative knowledge is of considerable value; for, as far as it goes, it is an argument for freedom of choice between different possibilities. Only if you are quite certain of what will happen, will you be prudent in giving society a cast-iron form; otherwise the best solution will be one admitting of easy adjustment to changing conditions.

It will hardly be questioned that the tendencies of the present time are all in the opposite direction. Restrictions on international trade, in order to prevent foreign competition to practically every activity, are the order of the day. Trades and occupations, threatened by changes in demand, are protected by the most drastic measures: witness the agricultural policy prevailing almost the world over. Private associations successfully close trades and occupations to newcomers.

Whether these tendencies will be able to prevent change is, I think, a question depending upon the strength of governments and private associations, on one side, and that of technological research and the business world's ability of improvement in industrial and commercial organization on the other. For, strong as are the powers working against change, they have not so far been able at all to check the tendency to a reshapement of economic life. This, as far as I am able to see, is the outcome of those forces I have just mentioned: the progress of technology and business organization. So long as that remains intact, a return to pre-nineteenth-century conditions will not take place. But if, for example, "rationalization" should be penalized—of which there have been some hints—and the work and ingenuity of scientists confined to purposes of destruction—which is not a very far-fetched idea, either—then the victory over the nineteenth century will have been achieved.

For technical and economic, as well as political, development has placed power in the hands of governments in a fashion unheard of in earlier times; and what was impossible of achievement in the field of government policy a century ago has now become an easy matter. Let me enlarge somewhat upon this—in my view fundamental but perpetually overlooked—fact by giving a few instances.

It has been said thousands of times that modern large-scale production has strengthened the hands of private capital, which is undoubtedly true. But as a matter of fact the same forces have strengthened the hands of governments to a much greater extent. Without it I do not think modern dictatorships would have been able to maintain half of the power they now wield. When a government of former

times wished to influence the opinions of its subjects, there were hardly more than two means at its
disposal, both of them weak. One was to issue
pamphlets and broadsheets, which only a small
minority of the population was able to read, whilst
few even of those who were able to read cared to
do so, preferring news of calves with two heads and
such-like things. The other, much more effective
measure, but very limited in scope nevertheless, was
to make speeches at fairs and other gatherings,
where governments would be exceptionally happy
if their spokesmen could find as many as one
thousand people present at the same time. I think
there can be no doubt that parish priests possessed far
greater opportunities for shaping the minds of their
parishioners than all the governments of the world.

All that has now changed. First, governments are
masters of the radio system, and broadcasting is the
veritable *biblia pauperum* of modern times, a Bible
of the Poor, accessible to all and capable of putting
across ideas that may be absorbed almost without
an effort. But a similar condition prevails in all
directions. In earlier times it was possible to keep
up the struggle of opinion with the help of small
printed sheets, the production of which was within
the means of many private individuals. Now, on the
other hand, the masters of the enormous kites which
are modern newspapers, issued by the million and
distributed throughout the country, turned out by
printing-presses immeasurably beyond the means
of ordinary people, can laugh at attempts of their

poor adversaries to fight them with small, clandes-
tine printing-presses; it would be like the fight
between a man armed with a bow and arrow and
a man in command of modern artillery. If a government once acquires mastery of the radio and the
press simultaneously, its power is, humanly speaking, secured against internal enemies. In several
places in his earlier books, Mr. H. G. Wells has
expressed his surprise that governments allow such
a powerful weapon over the mind as the newspaper
to remain in the hands of the capitalists. The dictators of to-day have taken his hint very seriously,
and it would be interesting to know whether Mr.
Wells considers their solution an improvement upon
conditions prevailing in countries still without dictatorship. However that may be, there can be no
shadow of a doubt that governments possess much
greater chances of using, or abusing, the modern
printing-press for their purposes than any private
capitalist.

In the more material fields, a comparison with
Napoleonic times is illuminating. Napoleon failed
signally in preventing, through his Continental
System, British goods from entering the Continent;
but the Allies in the Great War were fairly successful
in starving Central Europe into capitulation. In
earlier times it was considered impossible to prevent
gold from leaving a country where its price was
low; this was compared with "hedging the cuckoo";
and one of the principal reasons for abolishing the
prohibition of gold exports from England in the

seventeenth century was that it could not be enforced. Now it is enforced in almost every country,
and there is practically no leakage at all. Also international capital movements are at present almost
entirely under government control, as an outcome
of the modern systems of transportation, the post
and the telegraph in the first place; nothing like it
would have been possible in earlier days. All prohibitions in international trade before the era of
laissez-faire had to reckon with an enormous amount
of smuggling, which made the prohibitions function
as a comparatively modest form of import duties;
now, on the other hand, the command over the railways especially has enabled governments to reduce
smuggling to insignificant proportions, in spite of
a restrictive policy which bids fair to compete with
that of the pre-Liberal period.

Like all other human changes, this one, of course,
is psychological in its root. People have come to
believe in the wisdom of governments, at least as
uncritically as they suspected them before. It is the
same with regard to the rest of the hindrances to
change. Business men in the last century, like most
other people at the time, not only believed in "progress" with a capital P, and adapted themselves to
it—even in cases where their private interests would
have been better served by action of a different kind.
They further believed that "progress" was the outcome of individual action. Thus, I think, cartels and
fusions would have made greater progress than they
did before the war, if business men, under the

influence of a particular view of life, had not clung to individual action.

But since the war this tendency has completely changed. The former facile belief in "progress" has disappeared; under the influence of a host of new forces, spiritual and material; individual action has retained but few adherents; the majority in almost every class and department of life believe in government control, association, and monopoly.

To a great extent this is the outcome of technical and economic forces with their roots far back in the nineteenth century. During and just after the great Industrial Revolution of the eighteenth century, society, it is true, was more "atomistic" than perhaps ever before or since; and the belief of the classical economists, as well as most other educated people, in the reality of such situation, when only the trammels of government interference were set aside, had a certain foundation in actual fact.

But already at a comparatively early date new forces made themselves felt; it was the old story of Frankenstein's monster, the creature turning against its creator. First and foremost among these new creatures of nineteenth-century industrialism were the railways. A more rigid system of transportation has never been invented. Railway traffic is bound to follow tracks laid down for it beforehand and to stop at particular stations and termini, usually difficult to transfer to other places. Further, the "permanent way" is permanent indeed, and represents a considerable part of the total capital sunk in the railways; whilst the rolling stock, locomotives and cars, can only with difficulty be transferred to new uses. The result is an enormous preponderance of overhead costs, and high overhead costs are almost incompatible with competition, making almost invariably for monopoly. Thirdly, the size of the unit of transport, not only the train but also each separate unit, became much bigger than it had been in earlier types of transportation. It is true that this is a far more important factor in other countries than England, where the small goods trucks of the early railway period have often been retained, while most other countries have gone over to trucks of say twenty to forty tons capacity each. As a result, large "shippers" of goods have received a strong advantage over small "shippers" on account of cheaper rates available for full truck-loads.

The advent of the railway, in its turn, has reacted strongly upon industry, which for reasons of its own became also, though somewhat later, subjected to the same influences. Especially since the 1870's and 1880's production became more and more concentrated upon the "heavy" industries, creating fixed capital; also within the establishment of these industries fixed capital and overhead costs incessantly grew in importance, when compared with floating capital and with costs corresponding to output. The comparatively small textile factory, considered typical of early industrialism, has progressively lost importance in comparison with the ever-expanding concerns in iron and engineering. Cartels and trusts followed in their wake, and economic life had already, long before the war, travelled far from the atomistic society of the Industrial Revolution. But the final victory, that over men's minds, mainly belongs to the post-war period.

Now, just as *laissez-faire* retained its psychological sway long after it had ceased to dominate actual conditions, there is every reason to expect the same with regard to its conqueror. Even if economic life should show a tendency to turn away from the road laid for it in the later nineteenth century, it will take a long time before people come to understand it. But there is this vast difference between the two cases, that, whereas *laissez-faire* did and does nothing to prevent a development opposed to itself, the belief in interference and monopolistic organization consciously counteracts tendencies to change. Therefore the question as to which will prove the stronger will become of great practical importance, if such new tendencies should begin to show themselves.

Are tendencies of that character already afoot? I think they are, but do not by this affirm that they will be strong enough to supersede those of an opposite character. They are, however, for the greater part almost completely overlooked not only in popular discussion but also in the writings of economists, and I think there can be no doubt that they should be taken into account where our economic future is concerned.

A new form of land transportation has arrived: road traffic by motor. People now are apt to repeat the mistakes made on the arrival of the railway a century ago. The railway at the beginning was treated as a sort of canal, because that was the form of transport people knew and understood. For that reason small sections of road were allowed each railway company, so that trunk lines had to be pieced together from a whole bunch of separate grants. Particular rates were prescribed for the use of the line on the one hand, and for the use of the trains on those lines on the other, just as canal tolls were distinct from rates for the use of ships upon the canal, etc. All this had to be changed; but at the present moment road traffic is extensively treated according to the ideas derived from railway traffic, so that omnibus lines have to acquire licences—which are very frequently denied them—and their competition is restricted by every means. In actual truth the motor omnibus, economically speaking, represents a *pre*-railway type of concern, just as it shows a remarkable family likeness to the stage-coach of the days of Charles Dickens in its outward aspect.

It is almost amusing to think of the contrast between railway and motor traffic from an economic point of view. The unit is small instead of big; fixed capital is insignificant in comparison with floating capital; a flexible and adaptable form of land transportation has grown up alongside the rigid one. Motor traffic can begin and end anywhere and go from house to house; it can change its route as conditions require.

The change in the economic character of traffic itself is therefore clear; there is room for competition in motor traffic, whereas it is practically impossible in railway traffic. But the results do not end there. The traders also are influenced by it and will probably be more so when goods traffic becomes more important on the roads than it is now. For on the road the smallness of the unit enables the small producer to send for raw materials and send away his own goods as cheaply as the big producer, who is not favoured in motor as in railway traffic; even a comparatively small producer can become master of his own transport service by having his own vans. The smallness of the transport unit, moreover, gives a fillip to production on a small scale, by creating a need for small retail shops all over the country. That this opens up interesting possibilities everyone must admit.

There is one more new branch of transportation which from some points of view bears the same imprint to an even greater degree; that is air-craft. But, so far, air transport has not meant very much in goods traffic; and as that is the important consideration from the present point of view, air traffic had better be left aside in this connection.

However, there is also a widely different new force come to life, the importance of which is undeniable and which holds a very peculiar position. That is electric power. Its production is certainly on a very large scale, even larger than steam-power generation; but in spite of that it favours the small industrial unit. This arises from the very important fact of its being distributed over a large area, where it can be used as cheaply by the small as by the big industrial unit. Steam-power, on the contrary, must be used where it is generated; and as power generation, in this case also, is cheapened by increase in amount, steam-power assists the big industrial unit up to a rather high point.

The effects of the forces now under discussion are, of course, to a great extent music of the future, which appears excusable when our task precisely is to discuss the future. How great an influence these new forces have already had, in the direction now indicated, is not at all clear, though something may be said about it. Unfortunately, statistics of industrial production are usually in a very bad state; censuses are taken at arbitrary intervals, and little is done to make them comparable. This makes conclusions from them uncertain with regard to most countries.

Statistics of manufactures in Germany suffer more than those of most countries from lack of comparability from one date to another. It would therefore be idle to attempt any conclusions from the fact that the lowest group, the quite small units, in German industry shows a strong relative rise between 1925 and 1933, and the highest group, containing the greatest number of workers per establishment, a corresponding fall. Probably figures for manufactures in Great Britain and the United States are somewhat more comparable between censuses of production. They show, however, a decrease for the lowest group, that with the smallest number of workers per establishment, but a fall likewise for the highest group, or groups, with the largest number of workers per establishment. On an average there is little change either way, though mostly in the direction of an increase in size. But it is quite otherwise with regard to the only country I know where annual and absolutely uniform industrial statistics are being compiled and published. That country is Sweden; and I must therefore dwell a little longer upon her figures.

Between 1913 and 1930 the comparative number of workers in the lowest group, of no more than ten workers per establishment, grew very rapidly, from 5·8 to 8·5 per cent. The figures no doubt are small, but the relative increase, as will appear, very remarkable. The highest group, of more than one thousand workers per establishment, grew also; but the much stronger influence from the decrease in size comes out in the average, which fell from 39 workers per establishment in 1913 to 28 in 1935, surely no small fall. The tendency, besides, is absolutely uniform, occurring in all groups of industries. These results stand out more clearly when seen against the background of the pre-war period, 1896–1912, when developments were in every respect in the opposite direction. To a great extent the result is explained by an extended installation of (electric) power, exchanging the human factor for machinery. But even when this change is taken into consideration, there is a distinct decrease in size since the pre-war period.

But whether this undeniable tendency in Sweden has had a counterpart in the greater industrial countries is quite another question. I think it rather probable, but can give no proofs of my belief, so that no more can be said now than that developments should be watched much more closely than hitherto, and that censuses of all industrial production should be made more comparable between different years within each country than has until now been the case.

We are on much surer ground when studying another very important post-war movement, which by 1930 had already shown unequivocal results. It finds expression in changes in the occupations of the people. The results I am now going to produce refer to comparisons between the occupational censuses of 1920 and 1930 or adjacent years, in fourteen countries, among which are the principal industrial ones. This is the list: The United States; England and Wales; Scotland; Germany; Switzerland; Czechoslovakia; Italy; France; Canada; Japan; the Scandinavian countries; and Holland. The figures therefore are undeniably representative. They are to be found in the table on pages 100 and 101.

The first conclusion following from this comparison is far from surprising, but none the less very significant. It is a strong decrease in the share falling to agriculture as an occupation of the people. This

DISTRIBUTION ACCORDING TO OCCUPATIONS IN FOURTEEN COUNTRIES
IN 1920 AND 1930 (OR ADJACENT YEARS)*

Countries	Year	I Agriculture, Fishing, Forestry	II Industry, Handicrafts, Mining	III Commerce, Shipping, Transport generally	IV Public Services, Free Professions	V Household Work and Various	Total
Sweden ...	1920	40·7	31·0	14·3	5·6	8·4	100·0
	1930	35·6	31·7	17·5	6·3	8·9	100·0
Finland ...	1920	68·9	12·8	6·0	2·9	9·4	100·0
	1930	63·4	14·4	7·4	3·6	11·2	100·0
Norway ...	1920	36·8	29·0	19·7	5·1	9·4	100·0
	1930	35·3	26·5	21·8	5·7	10·7	100·0
England and Wales ...	1921	6·8	47·3	24·5	10·4	11·0	100·0
	1931	5·6	46·2	26·9	10·9	10·4	100·0
Scotland ...	1921	9·5	49·4	22·9	9·0	9·2	100·0
	1931	8·9	45·1	26·6	10·2	9·2	100·0
France ...	1921	41·5	29·9	16·6	8·1	3·9	100·0
	1926	38·3	33·2	17·1	7·4	4·0	100·0
Italy ...	1921	55·7	24·3	10·3	6·1	3·6	100·0
	1931	47·3	29·5	12·9	6·3	4·0	100·0
Holland ...	1920	23·6	37·4	21·3	8·2	9·5	100·0
	1930	20·6	38·1	23·4	8·6	9·3	100·0

Switzerland	1920	25·8	44·2	16·7	7·1	6·3	100·0
	1930	21·3	45·0	19·0	7·5	7·3	100·0
Germany	1925	30·5	42·1	16·4	6·6	4·4	100·0
	1933	28·9	40·4	18·4	8·4	3·9	100·0
Czechoslovakia	1921	33·7	40·5	10·9	7·9	7·0	100·0
	1930	28·3	42·2	13·6	8·5	7·4	100·0
United States	1920	26·3	33·4	18·3	6·9	15·1	100·0
	1930	22·0	30·9	21·1	8·5	17·5	100·0
Canada	1921	35·0	25·4	20·0	9·0	10·6	100·0
	1931	31·2	26·6	23·4	9·1	9·7	100·0
Japan	1920	53·8	21·0	15·5	5·4	4·3	100·0
	1930	50·4	18·9	19·1	6·9	4·7	100·0
Average	*Circa* 1920	35·1	33·2	16·8	7·1	7·8	100·0
	1930	31·3	33·1	18·4	8·3	8·9	100·0

* Source: *Statistical Year Book of the League of Nations.*—In the 1935 issue a somewhat detailed discussion of the character of the figures for different countries is to be found. Unless considerations of comparability have led to another treatment, figures refer to trades rather than to occupations proper. As the absolute percentages for different countries are very frequently not comparable, only their changes within each country should be taken into account.

result recurs in each of the fourteen countries, without exception. The average shows a fall from 35·1 to 31·3 per cent of total population, an unusually great change in no more than ten years. But it has been going on for a much longer time; e.g., in the United States the figure was 33 in 1910, 26 in 1920, and 22 in 1930.

The explanation is not far to seek. It consists in a combination between stagnant, or even diminishing, demand per head of population on one side, and increasing supply on the other side. The shrinking of demand, in its turn, is due to a rise in the standard of living, combined with a stagnant population. Long ago Adam Smith said: "The desire of food is limited in every man by the narrow capacity of the human stomach; but the desire of the conveniences and ornaments of building, dress, equipage, and household furniture, seems to have no limit or certain boundary." When people have enough to eat, they turn to the satisfaction of other wants, and every increase in income above that point tends to diminish the proportion of agriculture to total production, and the percentage of total population falling to it. If the number of mouths to be filled increases, this tendency may be counteracted; but otherwise it will continue as far as the rise in the standard of living. I am unable to see any change in the tendency under present conditions, unless there arises a new demand for food, and more particularly of European and American food, from countries where food consumption has been low and directed to non-cereals, such as the rice-consuming parts of Asia. If the industrialization of those parts proceeds, there will arise an exchange between their manufactures and the cereals of Europe and America —a curious inversion of earlier conditions. But as to whether that will in fact take place, I do not wish to express an opinion, as I know far too little of economic conditions in the East. If it does not take place, I see no escape from the decrease in agricultural population in Europe and America, whatever governments may do. It is quite true that this reasoning presupposes improvements in technique and methods of production generally in agriculture similar to those characteristic of industrial production; but that condition is amply fulfilled. Though the result as a whole was only to be expected, it throws a curious light upon the agricultural policy pursued by most countries.

Far more surprising, at least to myself, has been the next result, referring to industry (including mining, etc.) as one of the great occupational groups. There have been few facts discussed so much *ad nauseam* as the growing industrialization of the world during the last hundred or hundred and fifty years; everyone knows that the great labour movement of our time has also had its principal root in this. The result of a comparison between 1920 and 1930 is the remarkable one that this tendency has now altogether spent its force. On an average the percentage population occupied in industry was almost exactly the same in 1930 as in 1920: 33·2 per cent in 1920 and 33·1 in 1930. In the leading industrial countries, however, there was a distinct fall. For example, in the United States from 33·4 to 30·9—indeed a spectacular decrease in ten years; England and Wales much less but not inconsiderable, from 47·3 to 46·2, and in Scotland a very pronounced fall, from 49·4 to 45·1. On the other hand, some of the fourteen countries, such as Czechoslovakia, Italy, and Finland, which entered the movement towards industrialization at a somewhat later date, still show a considerable increase, while the rest have been fairly constant. This consequently shows a strong contrast to what has been going on for a long time.

On the other hand, this result is as far as possible from meaning that industrial production has decreased either absolutely or relatively. On the contrary, industrial production has grown by leaps and bounds; but it has become possible to achieve this increase in output by the labour of an unchanged or even a diminished percentage of the total population. The explanation may be given in the word "rationalization," though that is a misleading expression; for rationalization in the original sense of the word has been going on since the Stone Age. It had therefore better be translated into an increase in mechanization and organization, which has partly superseded men by machinery, and partly made better use of both men and machines. The remarkable thing is that the results have been so far-reaching in spite of an absence of epoch-making mechanical, metallurgical, or chemical inventions. Probably economic factors have been the most important ones, partly no doubt a greater insight into the different factors of production on the part of employers, but probably also a changed relation between labour cost and the cost of fixed capital, i.e., high wages and a low rate of interest.

The significance of the change in the industrial group of occupations becomes clear when the next occupational group is also considered, that of commerce and transport. The share falling to these occupations has increased between the years 1920 and 1930 from 16·8 to 18·4 per cent, on an average for the fourteen countries; the same tendency appears in every single country. These are the figures, for example, of the United States, 18·3 to 21·0 per cent; England and Wales, 24·5 to 26·9 per cent; and Scotland, 22·9 to 26·6—Scotland, by the way, generally showing the new tendencies in a particularly pronounced fashion.

There can thus be no doubt about the growing commercialization of the world—a sesquipedalian word, but difficult to avoid. In itself there is nothing new in the growth of the commercial group; the novelty consists in its continued growth simultaneously with the stagnation of the industrial population. How can this be possible, when commerce and transport handle the raw materials and finished products of industry in the first place? The first half of the answer to this question is that, while the industrial population has been at a standstill, its

production has increased enormously, so that there
have been much more goods to handle than formerly.
But why have commerce and transport needed an
increase in man-power, while it has not been necessary in the production of the commodities? This
is because the forces at work in industry, i.e.,
mechanization and organization, have had much
smaller scope in commerce and transport. But some
specific factors probably have also been at work.
For instance, the need for salesmanship certainly
increases with the rise in the general standard of
living, because purchasers must be treated more
intensively when having greater choice between the
satisfaction of wants that are not necessities, as well
as between different commodities to satisfy them;
differentiation of wants and commodities in itself
increases the work of marketing and selling. In the
field of transport the spread of the motor-car has
no doubt increased the relative need for man-power
as compared with capital.

There has also been a marked increase in the two
groups of "public services and free professions"
and "household and various work." But the second
of these two groups especially is so ill-defined
that it is difficult to say what this change really
means.

The growing commercialization of the world
comes to light also within industry itself. There it
is a growing need for salesmanship, organization
and central work, as well as technical ability, as
compared with pure manual work. The result has

been an even greater change within industry than that between industry and commerce. Partly, it may be expressed by saying that, besides the increase falling to commerce as an independent group, commercial activities take up much more time than before within the industrial concerns themselves. All this has produced a very marked increase in the number of non-manual workers in industry, not only absolutely but also in proportion to manual workers. This refers to all groups of non-manual workers, administrative, clerical, and technical. Only in 1936 it was made the subject of a particular investigation on the part of the International Labour Office at Geneva, and I shall in the main confine myself to giving a few figures from that survey.

Between the periods 1905–11, 1919–25, and 1929–34 (or thereabouts) the number of non-manual workers per 100 wage-earners (or manual workers), according to censuses of population, rose, for example, in Germany from 27·1 to 36·5 to 36·9; in France from 26·8 to 30·8 to 33·1; in Switzerland from 22·5 to 27·2 to 31·0. According to censuses of production (in manufacturing) the figures rose, for example, in the United States from 11·9 to 15·9 to 15·4—a slight fall this time; in Great Britain from 7·6 to 9·5 to 11·3; in Canada from 8·6 to 15·8 to 16·9, etc. As usual, figures for manufactures in Sweden could be given for each year, but it may be enough to give them for the periods 1913–15, 1926–30, and 1935: from 8·9 to 10·9 to 13·0. Absolute increase for each group may, however, be added in this case. If the figures for 1913 are in each case put at 100, the number of clerical employees in 1935 had risen to 166, but the technical ones to no less than 312, as against a rise in wage-earners to no more than 131. With regard to Sweden, the increase in technical staff is still as strong as it ever was, while that of clerical workers appears now to have stagnated in relative, though not in absolute, figures, on account of a strong increase in the number of wage-earners in the course of the boom of the last few years.

As will easily be seen, this change in the character of industrial employees is in perfect harmony with the new relation between industry and commerce. It shows a strong growth in what may be called the lower middle class and a corresponding relative decrease in the working class in the old sense of the word. If the tendency to relative growth in the number of the smaller industrial units will also materialize, a third factor will work in the same direction.

I therefore think that certain new forces are afoot, tending to change modern society from the form created by the forces of the later nineteenth century, but that these new forces differ a great deal from what is usually laid down in public discussion, both by the general public and by the economists; and I submit that they be taken into account when considering our economic future. As to the degree of importance they will achieve in the future, I do not wish to express an opinion. But as they are in my view more to the good than to the bad, I think that room should be found for them, and that they should not be strangled in their cradle by measures against economic change, actuated by governments, private associations, or class interests.

V

MENTAL SETTINGS OF OUR ECONOMIC FUTURE

by S. DE MADARIAGA, M.A.

I. SCIENCE AND PROPHECY

FORECAST of the future is the hallmark of scientific achievement. It is so for utilitarian reasons; short of it, science becomes a mere intellectual game and as such can only appeal to fully grown-up minds, for not till we grow up do we realize that useful things are but tools for achieving and enjoying the useless; it is so for reasons of method, since till it is made to "work," i.e. to fit future events as well as past ones, a scientific theory is no more than a guess or adumbration; but it is so for more profound and less rationalistic motives, because man's deepest desire is to widen and deepen his power over nature, which in practice means his hold over events to come, a faculty which fills his soul with an all but divine satisfaction, since it gives him the illusion of tasting the joy of creation.

The sense of unity is the other deep motive which drives man on the path of scientific discovery. Though our era be one of dispersion and analytical research, though the all-round science of old may now have branched off into "sciencelets," cultivated by swarms of experts, the mind of man behind all these specialists seeks a unity for all that; a unity in things, which may reduce them all to a general principle; and a unity between things and man, since that general principle, it is assumed, would be in harmony with the laws which regulate human thought.

The two impulses meet at this point. For, while this desire to reduce all things to a principle of human thought may seem disinterested in its intellectual detachment, psychologists are entitled to see in it one of the many forms of man's sense of power. Detachment and objectivity are not virtues of the mind; they are mere rules of the game, or better still, rules for the use of the mental apparatus, in fact part of the apparatus itself. But the aim of the man who uses the apparatus is obviously the widening and deepening of his power—either for the sake of the fruits of power or for the pleasure to be found in power itself.

The majesty of religion shifted to science when its magic did. For the lay masses, the scientist is but the modern form of the wizard. During a period —which we had thought definitive but now know to have been but a brief phase—science had over religion the advantage, if advantage it was, of a clear and transparent doctrine, altogether lacking in mysteries. Yet, we may say of nature's mysteries what Bacon said of the Gods; knowledge drove them away, more knowledge brings them back. The lay masses who saw the wizard in the scientist because he performed the miracle, are now the more justified in that few human beings can understand how the miracle is performed. Of the two motives of science, the urge to unity is therefore doomed to remain for ever unsatisfied in all but a small number of privileged minds; and so the capacity to forecast the future becomes for most of us the only scientific achievement which we can grasp.

From this point of view, mathematics, the most perfect of sciences, is but a play of the mind, or a tool of the science of things, or a set of the laws of the intellect. Mathematics may be interpreted as a special notation of the easiest branch of psychology —that which studies the working of the mind unpolluted by emotions. But mathematics is born of experience, if only of mental experience; and the history of science offers many cases in which the physicist has created a demand for mathematical concepts which the mathematician had to satisfy.

We meet here for the first time that interaction between the mind and nature which our age seems to have for its special mission to describe and to emphasize. The most abstract of our concepts are steeped in concrete experience; just as the matter-of-fact peasant who answers *"straight* ahead" to the enquiries of the motorist is using perfectly abstract language, since he does not refer to the actual shape of the road, which may be far from "straight," but to the concept of it as that which does not fork either to the right or to the left. Mathematics, the science of abstractions, is the science of *our* abstractions, of those we need as we advance further and further into the virgin forests of nature.

That such a collaboration between mind and nature is at the basis of physical observation was well known. It is admirably emphasized in the difficulty which most of us experience when we try to represent what the eye sees without the mind meddling with the vision; as shown in the fact that in the case of most children the capacity for drawing deteriorates as the mind develops; indeed, the art of painting is built up on the wide margin left for the vagaries of the mind and for the variety of temperament and interpretation round the naked object which is actually there—an object which no one can see as it actually is.

But not till Einstein did we realize how deep is this meddling of the mind with the object in our so-called objective study of physical nature. Copernicus himself had not corrected our incorrigible conceit. Einstein has shown us that our concepts of space and time are dependent on the fact that the motions which we had so far observed were but slow, and that space and time melt into each other like sky and sea when the speed of the object rises to magnitudes comparable with the speed of light. What is more to the point, thanks to Einstein, the facts of physics are now seen to occur in a space-time flux in which the present is no longer a rigid conception but one dependent on the frame of reference, or clock, or observer reporting the events.

When we were just getting used to the new posture which our minds had thus to adopt as to movement, Planck's famous discovery of quantum-mechanics came to remove one other of the bases of our thought, this time in the field of force. Reversing the old tag—*natura non facet saltum*—already badly shaken in biology by the theory of mutations, Planck showed that nature works only by leaps. From stationary stage to stationary stage, atoms pass by definite steps, not by a continuous gradient, but as one ascends or descends a flight of stairs. All efforts at conciliating this view with the old "wave" or electromagnetic view of light, so brilliantly justified by many an experiment, have proved useless.

The deadlock is viewed in divers ways by the chief wizards of our day. For Mr. Einstein it simply proves that quantum-mechanics does not suffice to give an accurate and complete description of physical reality. But for Mr. Niels Bohr, it merely points to "the necessity of a final renunciation of the classical idea of causality and a radical revision of our attitude towards the problem of physical reality.[1] This far-reaching change in the "posture" of our mind, which for Mr. Niels Bohr is similar to that demanded of us by the theory of relativity, flows from "the impossibility of controlling the reaction of the object on the measuring instrument if these are to serve their purpose."

May we now stop for breath? Here we are in a world within and without which lives in and through us. We try to grasp it. We begin with the facts of

---

[1] "Can Quantum-mechanical Description of Physical Reality be Considered Complete?" by Niels Bohr, *Physical Review* (U.S.A.), October 15, 1935.

physics. They are the simplest, for here is the mind on one side and here is nature on the other, and all we need do is to measure without and to think within. Such was the simplicity of the problem until not so long ago. But in our day it has become more complicated. Our means are three: senses, concepts, tools. Our senses get mixed up with our concepts; our concepts with our tools; our tools with nature. What can we know? And can we know at all?

II. ECONOMICS AND PROPHECY

That is precisely what many of us had been wondering with regard to political economy. Can it be considered as a science at all? How can it, we answer, when the observers are plunged in the mass of the observed, when the mind which thinks and the matter which is thought are one and the same, when measurements disturb the facts which are measured and influence the yardsticks, when "systems" cannot be isolated for observation out of the seething magma of events? And so we viewed political economists and sociologists as pariahs in the world of science, for ever denied access at the Santa Sanctorum of Exact Knowledge.

And now we see the distance between sciences so-called exact and what we might then have described as the hankering sciences suddenly reduced not by the achievement of the economist but by the modesty of the physicist. His ordeal in the arcana of the atom has sobered his ambitions. Nothing more striking than the frequent use of the word *renunciation* in the vocabulary of some of them.[1] Nature is not going to give away all its secrets. Man may catch a glimpse here and a glimpse there; he may, for instance, make a consistent description of the space-time pattern of physical life; he may also make a consistent description of the energy-momentum pattern of physical life. He must, however, give up all hope of combining the observation of these two aspects of nature since they mutually exclude themselves from measurement.

I have neither the competence nor the wish to participate in the controversy over these views amongst physicists, beyond suggesting that this conclusion to which some of them are led is of the utmost interest for political economists and sociologists. The facts which we have to observe are to an even greater extent interwoven with human preconceptions, prepossessions, prejudices, and presuppositions; they depend even more so than do physical facts on the observer; but, above all, they seem to be composed of two entirely different kinds of nature which may be described as the psychological and the statistical. Just as physical phenomena may be seen either under the space-time pattern or under the energy-momentum pattern, so economic and general sociological facts may be seen under the statistical and under the psychological pattern. Without in any way stressing the similarity beyond the

[1] Notably, Mr. Niels Bohr in *Atomic Theory and the Description of Nature*, Cambridge University Press, 1934.

bounds of a mere metaphor, it may even be said that in sociology and economics the statistical and the psychological aspects are as mutually exclusive as are the space-time and the momentum-energy aspects in physical nature.

Two more remarks on this point. Physical facts bearing on other than microscopic masses and small velocities are covered by the laws of classical mechanics, just as usual economic transactions of small importance are covered by the laws of classical economics; and, to complete this arresting parallel, the trend of atomic physics would appear to be to interpret the space-time pattern, through the electro-magnetic theory, in the form of wave-mechanics and statistical laws; and to visualize the momentum-energy pattern in the form of crowds of loose particles endowed with a definite individual behaviour — whether or not endowed also with a certain indetermination and free choice matters less for our present purpose and would take us on to a somewhat fanciful and dangerous field.

The temptation is therefore great—let us be moderate and resist its more alluring snares—to discover here yet another of those glimpses of unity in nature which are either the higher beacon of man's pilgrimage or else (who knows?) "the last infirmity of noble minds." For economy and sociology are also made up of space-time events coming in waves (including the famous *cycles*) and subject to statistical laws; and yet, simultaneously, of the doings of human individuals behaving as they please, or so they think, within certain limits set to their liberty. And if the parallel may be fitted with a practical conclusion, could we not, on the authority of our brethren the physicists, "renounce" all hope of reducing psychology to statistics and statistics to psychology, and boldly go forward along the two parallel roads, exploring the two mutually exclusive aspects of our collective nature?

Hardly uttered, this remark sounds already curiously heretical. Not, I trust, that heresy is inherent in it, but when there are so many dogmas about, heresy is almost inevitable. One is always a heretic for somebody and in our unfortunate age one is at times a heretic for everybody. Our age is precisely one in which most people insist *both* on the subjective character of *all* ideas on collective life, and on the absolute dogmatic value of such ideas when they happen to be their own. While we propose that the statistical aspect of collective life should be allowed to develop in peace, free from psychological meddling, and that collective psychology should be cultivated in itself, without undue regard for statistics; thus giving an objective, but only a relative, value to our economic and sociological thought.

This discipline is more necessary in the economic and sociological than in the physical field. For our human "particles," though more deeply sunk than they imagine in the "wave-economics" or space-time pattern of events, are nevertheless incomparably more powerful than mere atoms and far richer in initiative.

Moreover, in so far as their ideas form a part of the social texture and movement, our particles, individual men, create in part that reality which it is our object to study; they transform it, react to and are acted upon by observers. If one last parallel with physics be permitted, economics, thought observing thought, is like optics, light observing light, a science in which interaction of observer and observed is often bound to lead to ambiguity and at times to sheer darkness.

III. THE FIVE MENTAL SETTINGS

Would that these obvious facts were better known to the exponents of the several dogmas which now occupy the political field. For, as it happens, economic life has never been more upset than since it became conscious. In the old days men carried on their business without realizing that they were performing economic functions, very much as Molière's *Bourgeois Gentilhomme* spoke in prose. Then a kind of humdrum system, unaware of itself, set in and "took charge." Trouble began when, with the advent of economics as a science, liberalism entered the field. It assumed that, though individuals could err, the wave-mechanics of collective life was infallible. This error was short-lived, and led to such heavy sins on the part of some particles endowed with too much financial momentum and not enough moral weight, that it gave rise by a kind of reaction to the doctrine nowadays known as Marxism. In its present historical context, Marxism has fostered the counter-reaction known as nazism and fascism. Cutting across these mental attitudes the old reliance on the three religious virtues comes again to the fore. Finally, a kind of ethics of internationalism comes at times to simplify, at times to complicate, the debate.

One thing is certain. Our future, economic and general, is black unless these dogmas, and particularly the most rigid of them—fascism and communism—do not grow wiser and less dogmatic, which amounts to saying, do not disappear or commit suicide. For, apart from the direct action which our mental settings may have on economic life, the mere fact of the feud between fascism and communism, every day more vociferous and every day more capable of backing their vociferations with violence, is enough to keep the world in that state of fear of impending disaster which is the worst mental setting for economic life.

(1) *Liberalism*. — But apart from their mutual opposition these several settings of our economic life deserve close study, since they are bound to exert a powerful influence, at any rate on the psychological "aspect" of it. Economic liberalism as an unqualified policy is now dead and gone. Was it ever fully lived up to? We may doubt it. Even at the height of the Manchester school, even in the so-called free trade countries, restrictions which are inseparable from complete liberalism existed; for instance, in the matter of importation of foreign

labour. The conditions of modern economics do not admit of its application, again, as an unqualified doctrine; but it might be well to define, so to speak, the maximum and minimum of its utility under any circumstances and the deep-lying reason which makes of this doctrine of the past, if properly defined, an essential element of the doctrine of the future.

A maximum has always been set to liberalism by all the circumstances of collective life which spring either from the nature of the things handled, or from that of objective relations between men. This maximum has been bigger than it is to-day; but though the scope allowed to liberalism has shrunk considerably during the last one hundred years, the scope was at no time unlimited.

There are probably two kinds of limits, or, better, perhaps, two kinds of aspects of these limits: one flowing from economic considerations; one from other than economical considerations. The first, due to the fact that *homo economicus* does not perhaps altogether fit *homo manchesterianus;* the second to the fact that *homo sapiens* is far more complex than *homo œconomicus.* The first, on analysis, would probably be found to be connected with what we have described as wave-economics; the second with the quantum-mechanics of the human particles of society. The fluctuations which these limits undergo in the course of time are determined partly by the change in the material environment, due mostly to inventions, partly by the changes in the mental setting of the day.

Yet, it is worth noticing that, whatever these limits, a certain minimum of economic liberalism has always been respected. This minimum has been everywhere bigger than it is now; but, just as in free trade countries limits were set to liberalism in the freest days, so even in the most totalitarian countries (Soviet Russia, Nazi Germany, Fascist Italy) a limit is set by nature to the repression of liberalism, let alone the fact that the vigour of the repression is a measure of the vigour of the liberalism which is repressed under it.

For, in fact, there is in economic liberalism a kernel of indestructible truth which may be repressed and compressed but not suppressed. It embodies the belief in natural laws, the faith in the automatic processes of nature to restore its balance which it itself disturbs in the act of living. Liberalism was a policy justified by history as a phase in the liquidation of a past which had become obsolete to both things and thoughts; as a doctrine, it was too mechanical in its outlook and failed to realize that there were other aspects in nature besides that which it emphasized. But when we come to formulate the optimum mental setting which we wish fostered for the sake of our economic future, we will have occasion to point to liberalism as the heart and soul of the new school.

Liberalism, however, did not only fail because of its theoretical shortcomings as a doctrine; it failed mostly because of the sins which were committed in its name. Based on enlightened self-interest, it failed because self-interest is not always enlightened. And this remark ushers in a general observation; mental settings are unfortunately quite different in practice from what they appear to be in theory, and always unfavourably so, since the difference is due to the wear and tear of life and to the tendency of man to divert doctrines, as well as everything else, to his own selfish views.

(2) *Communism.*—This tendency is particularly well illustrated in the mental setting developed under communism. The school of Karl Marx may be considered as the chief rival of liberalism, which it calls capitalism. Liberalism emphasizes the human particle; communism emphasizes the "wave," which it calls the "masses" or the "proletariat." Built up of individual and of collective forces, society was bound to produce these two rival schools, and therefore communism was bound to act in history as a healthy antagonistic force enabling the community to keep its balance, upset by unchecked liberalism. It might be argued, without indulging in paradox, that in so far as liberalism rests on faith in the capacity of the body politic to keep its balance, it should consider communism as a confirmation of this faith, since communism is a healthy automatic reaction to restore the balance of the body politic compromised by an intransigeant liberalism. This being so, the intransigeance of communism turns out to be but the reflection of liberal intransigeance.

Nor is this the only case in which communism appears as the inverted image of liberalism. We may, indeed, restate about communism the very words already applied to liberalism: it is a policy justified by history as a phase in the liquidation of a past which had become obsolete to both things and thoughts; as a doctrine it is too mechanical in its outlook and fails to realize that there are other aspects in nature besides those which it emphasizes. Nor is it to be denied that when we come to examine the mental setting which we wish fostered for the sake of our economic future, the creative and positive side of communism will, as a matter of course, have to be incorporated in our outlook.

Further, communism, like liberalism, fails both in its theoretical shortcomings and in the application which is made of them. Its theory is too incoherent and dogmatic to be taken seriously by any scientific economist without political ambitions. It is bad economy and worse psychology. An economy built on pure Marxism is doomed to evolve back to some type of canalized capitalism, or perish in distress, or be maintained under a tyrannous rule. As for the effect of Marxist lore, it is curiously similar to that of liberalism; just as liberalism is an honourable cloak for all kinds of capitalistic tyranny, so communism is a cloak for all kinds of working-class tyranny and of most unpleasant demagogy on the part of Marxist leaders. The transformation of the notion of working persons (nearly everybody works nowadays) into that of "the working classes" and of the working classes into "the proletariat," is a piece of brazen insincerity based in democratic countries on shameless vote-catching impulses, of which socialist leaders should be ashamed.

(3) *Fascism.*—The counter-reaction to the communistic reaction against capitalism and liberalism is fascism. Both liberalism and communism are respectable. They may have their shortcomings, their bias, their illusions, and their vices; but they are respectable doctrines. Fascism is not respectable. We mean no offence and are only referring to its intellectual worth. True, in the long run it may be found to have rendered service by drawing attention to the importance of hierarchy and discipline. Yet fascism is a hotch-potch of adulterated guild-socialism (a most interesting doctrine when genuine), of Machiavellism, and of economic and military nationalism. As what we might describe as philosophic bunting, fascism spreads out Roman imperial splendours in Italy and Teutonic myths in Germany. Such a set of incoherent elements can only be held together by outside pressure, and in all known cases this pressure is fairly formidable. Fascist regimes keep a jealous watch lest their badly welded system suffers from the corrosive attacks of thought. This feature would suffice to brand them as dangerous to our economic future, for everything may be said about the future except that it can flourish in an atmosphere of confined thought.

But fascism is responsible for the worst feature of our mental setting, i.e. nationalism. Neither liberalism nor communism are originally and inherently tainted with nationalism. Both have acquired it as a contagion from fascism. Not that short-sighted and anti-liberal policy was unknown before fascism rose as a counterblast to communism; such a policy was indeed all too frequent and should figure amongst the causes of our troubles in the present and of our fears for the future; nor that communism in its only authenticated case was ever free from economic nationalism, as indeed it could not be, surrounded with capitalist nations which, to its infant eyes, must have looked like hungry wolves ready to devour the baby bear; but that the Fascist States, led by the method of their madness, were bound to shut themselves up in an autarchical policy, and so force most other States to a reactionary attitude in matters of foreign trade.

These three ways of thinking are the main tendencies which actually determine the mental setting of our economic future. They are all obsolete, irreconcilable, incomplete, dogmatic, and relatively simple. That is perhaps why they appeal so much to the vast majority of human beings, who seem to have an inveterate attraction for the cut and dried, the definite, the absolute, and who love an attitude of "either this or that."

(4) *The Religious Tendency.*—Two other currents cut across them, in fact *above* them, and complicate the picture: one is the tendency to offer the religious answer to the economic quest; the other is the tendency to internationalism. The first is irrelevant; the second is incomplete.

To be sure, if a genuine religious feeling were

more widespread amongst us, economic problems would be easier to solve. The suaveness of religious souls would put a new smoothness into the machinery. But the machinery would remain; the problem of how to modify present economic relations and change them into what they should be, considering the circumstances, would still be unsolved. Economic relations might be smoother without being right. Why!—it will be argued—if you ask me to walk one mile and I walk two, am I not solving all your problems? Of course you are not, because what is wanted in a healthy economic life is that when the competent man asks you to walk one mile, you should walk one mile; if you walk two, you will make a nuisance of yourself. Let there be no mistake about it; holiness is a category in itself; it will grace the inward life of a man; but, to borrow our language from geometry, the projection of a saint on the plane of economics is the right man in the right place doing the right thing at the right time; and none of these four "rights" has anything to do with religion.

The main tenet of religious faith—the belief in the common spiritual origin of man, and therefore the unity of human society—will, of course, be present in our ultimate construction. But, of its own, as an isolated and absolute proposition, religion is no answer to our economic problem.

(5) *Internationalism.*—Nor is mere internationalism as such. For the well-meant endeavour to enlarge the scope of national affairs to the international field

is more often than not a mere urge or blind instinct, or even an intellectual transposition of the images and impressions gathered by well-travelled persons in these days of perpetual motion; while for lack of a consistent and definite vision, of an intelligent conception of the world-trend, of a clear-sighted realization of the obstacles in the way, of a bold and courageous acceptance of the all but revolutionary changes which it implies, internationalism is often little more than a smug complacency over the cordial way we deal with mere foreigners, just as if they were like us.

IV. MENTAL ANARCHY AND THE WAY OUT

It is difficult to see how our economic future can flourish in peace—as, indeed, in peace it *would* flourish—when the world is in so appalling a state of mental anarchy. After all, nothing is either good or bad, but thinking makes it so; the Germans threaten war and thunder because they are reduced to a state of want which for the Spaniards would be plenty, indeed, indigestion; the workmen of our day strike to better conditions which would have seemed like a dream to their brethren of a hundred years ago; the heel of Stalin is freedom to the sons of the slaves who groaned under the Tsar's boot. There is not one world, there are at least five; the liberal, the communist, the fascist, the religious, the international—let alone the real world *an sich* which carries on under laws as indifferent to our thinking as the planet's movements to our jazz.

Is it not evident that the task of that leadership which Professor Condliffe rightly calls duty, is to put some order in our mental anarchy? Much as we may wish to consider as separate aspects of life its statistics and its psychology, our individual par ticles differ from electrons in that they can grasp, if not the whole system, at least the existence of a system to be grasped.[1] Their thought, if tuned up to unison in a number of them high enough to acquire a mass or wave character, is bound to influence the whole, this way or that. Stability, that longed-for ideal of an unstable age, by which we merely mean movement without jerks, flow without cataracts, stability depends mostly on the mass and momentum of our community which gives a certain consistency to its "wave-mechanics" and makes it possible to register statistical variations by means of relatively simple curves; but it depends also on the amplitude of the mental differences within the community.

In order to reduce these differences, something more definite is required than a mere compromise; amongst other reasons because no compromise is possible between the absolute and dogmatic attitude into which the mass, misled by its misleaders, is being polarized. This something may be defined both negatively and positively.

Negatively it means that all dogmatic positions must be given up. There are at least two reasons

[1] I apologize for this, the most unwarranted assumption in these pages, that electrons cannot think. For aught *we* know . . .?

I

for this: the first comes from the fact that no school of political economy can ever fit all the facts all the time. In other words, even more definite, there is no rigid *general* truth outside logic and its special language, mathematics. A few years ago we might have added physics. To-day our physicists beg us not to do so. When physicists "renouncing" objective knowledge seek refuge in relativity and in *complementarity*, how can economists, whether Marxist or liberal, dare be dogmatic? Of all the evils of the present, so fertile in them, none more deplorable than the sight of competent economists leading well-meaning and idealistic masses to dogmatic positions which the leaders are bound to know to be wrong as theory and dangerous as policy.

The second reason why dogmatic positions must be given up is the dual aspect of collective facts: they spring from the "free" actions of individuals, but, on the other hand, these individuals are so many that they also obey the same kind of wave-mechanics. Our dogmas act on the facts; the facts on our dogmas. Our dogmas, indeed, are part of the facts over which they dogmatize.

So much for the negative aspect of the mental setting we are seeking in order to ensure that our economic future flourishes in peace. As for its positive aspect, the new mental setting must be able to absorb all those we have described; though not a compromise between them, it must be a synthesis of all of them. Within its ambit, the liberal, the communist, the fascist, the religious-minded, and the internationalist, must be able to say: "That is what I meant." Freedom without anarchy, sense of the community without collective tyranny, national service without national idolatry, the civil substance of all religious faiths, and a concrete and constructive conception of world affairs—such are the conditions which our mental setting must fulfil. But all of them, by way of consequence. For, essentially, it must be something of its own.

V. COLLECTIVE LIFE IS LIFE

It is difficult to see how human community can be anything but a biological fact. Biologists are nowadays inclined to see in a hive or an anthill some kind of *being*. Why they have taken so long to be so inclined is a mystery. An association of beings of the same species which lives in as rigid a solidarity and reproduces itself with such definite laws as a beehive is a being, albeit not an individual being. A human community is a being.

To be sure it is not an organism in the sense in which a tree or an animal is an organism; but it is one for all that, or, if the word be denied by its present holders, it is something *sui generis* which is best understood by reference to an organism. It follows that life in a human community is but one, and that only by merely intellectual operations such as analysis and abstraction can we discriminate between the life of its individuals and the life of the community.

The extent and intensity of collective life depends mostly on the extent and intensity of the means of mental and physical communication within the community. In our time, the human community covers the whole world.

The human community is no exception to the biological rule that organisms are more and more diversified and richer in differentiated and specialized organs and tissues as they rise in the scale of life. Nowadays, the human community is highly diversified and specialized. It has several races; a score of different civilizations; threescore nations, and at least three natural classes of men: the instinctive, the intellectual or technical, and the intuitive or creative. Of the first, the masses are made; of the second, the middle classes; of the third, the leaders.

This system of natural classes tends both to coincide with that of the social classes (peasants, middle class, aristocracy) and to divert from it owing to the wear and tear of life and to the corruption which inevitably sets in in the two higher classes of society.

The most elementary study of economic facts leads nowadays to the conclusion that one and only life runs through all the limbs, organs, tissues, classes, nations, races of mankind. Definite separation, sharp, cut-and-dried frontiers are unthinkable. Those who think them as existing are the victims of intellectual delusions, unless they are led astray by the language. Thus, *heart*, *liver*, and *brain* are useful words, but as tangible and separate things they only exist at the butcher's. In the animal alive they do not exist; they are mere anatomical abstractions, not separate entities. Similarly, in diplomacy, in geography, we may speak of France, Germany, Italy. In world life they do not exist as separate entities and cannot even be thought of as forms of life apart from Great Britain, Holland, or Japan.

This being so, all entities below the whole, i.e. below the World Commonwealth, are but limbs of it. If they want the whole to keep them alive, they must live for the whole. Men and nations must realize inwardly—not merely think and agree—but *digest* and live—the unity of all this vast body politic which is mankind. No definite political organization need be associated with this vision; time and space will model such details. No uniform conception of the forms of collective life can be extended to the whole planet without grotesque inadequacies and tragic failures. But the fundamental unity of it all, the fact that there is only one life, must be realized everywhere, at any rate by the leaders.

Within this mental setting the future of mankind —including its economic future—will gradually evolve towards that active form of peace which pulsates in healthy beings. Liberalism will then have come into its own, since a number, possibly most of the motions and exchanges of collective life, can only be constantly readjusted by automatic processes which imply liberty. The substance of communism will be saved, for the health and wealth of the body politic will be the guiding principles under which such free exchanges and motions will tend to take place. Fascism will have saved its main positive contribution—the reinstatement of hierarchy and differentiation in the body politic. The religious tendency will find satisfaction in the recognition of the unity of men and nations under one harmonious and self-conscious mankind. And internationalism will have found its true goal and inspiration in the vision of a world of nations and men, more organic, more conscious of itself, more capable of achievement and order, than a mere co-operative of national egoisms. Nor should this mental setting be considered in any way as detracting from the dignity of the human individual soul; since, though every man's destiny be his own, our destinies are also the limbs of the destiny of mankind.

For Product Safety Concerns and Information please contact our EU
representative GPSR@taylorandfrancis.com
Taylor & Francis Verlag GmbH, Kaufingerstraße 24, 80331 München, Germany

www.ingramcontent.com/pod-product-compliance
Lightning Source LLC
Chambersburg PA
CBHW061332220326
41599CB00026B/5142